William Woodings

The Conduct and Management of parliamentary Elections

A practical Manual

William Woodings

The Conduct and Management of parliamentary Elections
A practical Manual

ISBN/EAN: 9783337163389

Printed in Europe, USA, Canada, Australia, Japan

Cover: Foto ©Lupo / pixelio.de

More available books at **www.hansebooks.com**

THE

CONDUCT AND MANAGEMENT

OF

PARLIAMENTARY ELECTIONS.

A PRACTICAL MANUAL.

BY

WILLIAM WOODINGS,

Assistant Secretary of the Liberal Central Association, London.

SOUTH COUNTIES PRESS LIMITED,
LEWES, SUSSEX.

1892.

CONTENTS.

ELECTION TIME TABLE.

MATTERS TO BE ATTENDED TO BY THE
CANDIDATE.

Immediately vacancy is declared and selection confirmed.

> Appoint Election Agent.
>
> Provide funds for Election expenses, and instruct Agent to open account.
>
> Prepare address to Electors.

On or before nomination day.

> Give notice in writing to Returning Officer of name and address of Election Agent.

On nomination day.

> Attend and deliver nomination papers to the Returning Officer.

Before the opening of the poll.

> Make declaration of secrecy before the Returning Officer or a Justice of the Peace.

Within 14 days after the day on which the result of the Election is declared.

> Prepare and forward to Election Agent a statement of the amount of his personal expenses as paid by himself; and if his personal expenses exceed £100, all bills in respect of such excess, and money to enable the Election Agent to pay the claims.

Within 35 days after the declaration of the result or within 7 days after the Election Agent has made his return and declaration as to expenses.

Transmit to the Returning Officer a declaration as to Election expenses made by himself before a Justice of the Peace; *or, if abroad, transmit the same within fourteen days after his return to the United Kingdom.*

MATTERS TO BE ATTENDED TO BY THE
ELECTION AGENT.

On receiving his appointment.

Open an " Election Expenses Account " at a Bank.
Print and circulate Candidate's address to the Electors.
Secure committee-rooms.
Appoint sub-agents (in counties), clerks, and messengers.
Prepare canvass books and district registers.
Arrange for special canvass of outvoters and removals
Form Election Committee.
Prepare scheme of meetings, and secure speakers.
Obtain nomination papers and see that they are filled up and signed.

On day of nomination.

Attend with the Candidate at place of nomination, and tender security (if required) for Returning Officer's charges.

At or immediately after delivery of nomination papers.

Object (if it is intended to do so) to any nomination open to objection on the ground of description of candidate being insufficient or not in compliance

with Rule 6 of the Ballot Act within the two hours
appointed for the nomination, or within one hour
afterwards.

Object to nomination papers on other valid grounds.

**Immediately the polling stations are fixed by the
Returning Officer.**

Print polling cards,

Direct envelopes for the same, and

Prepare any enclosures that are to be sent with the cards.

Arrange with postmaster as to time of posting cards, or
with local committees for delivery if they are not
to be sent by post.

One clear day at least before the polling day.

Give notice in writing to the Returning Officer of the
names and addresses of sub-agents.

Appoint counting agents, and give notice in writing to
the Returning Officer of their names and addresses.

At the same time appoint personation agents, and send
to the Returning Officer their names and addresses, and particulars as to the polling stations to
which they are appointed.

Before the opening of the poll.

Make declaration of secrecy before the Returning
Officer or a Justice of the Peace, and see that
the Candidate and all personation agents and
counting agents do the same.

See that outvoters and removals canvass is completed,
and that the marked lists for personation agents
are prepared, and, with their instructions, delivered
to them.

Also, that canvass cards are ready, vehicles allotted to

their districts, and all other arrangements completed for bringing voters to the poll.

Issue final instructions to sub-agents or clerks.

Immediately after the day on which the result of the Election is declared.

Publish notice to creditors to send in claims.

Within 14 days after the day on which the result of the Election is declared.

Receive all claims, including statements by sub-agents or others authorized to incur expenditure on account of petty expenses, and statement by Candidate as to his personal expenses.

Prepare and deposit his own claim for remuneration.

Within 21 days after the day on which *the return of Election is made.*

Receive detailed account of Returning Officer's charges.

Within 28 days after the day on which the result of the Election is declared.

Pay all claims not disputed.

Within 35 days after the day on which the result of the Election is declared.

Transmit to the Returning Officer the return of Election expenses, and declaration respecting the same.

Also see that the Candidate transmits his declaration in due course.

COUNTIES.

GENERAL.

ONLY those who have been practically engaged Changes. in election work, and who have had a varied experience, can appreciate the great changes which have taken place during the last few years in the method of conducting Parliamentary elections. The Corrupt Practices Act of 1883 introduced many legal changes; but these were hardly more important in their effect than the general changes involved in the extension of Household Suffrage to the Counties and the accompanying Redistribution of Seats.

The principle of popular representative organi- Represen-tative Associa-tions. zation, with which Mr. Schnadhorst is so closely identified, and which, under the nickname of "The Caucus," greatly alarmed a section of the community a few years ago, had already made some progress in the county constituencies; but its adoption after the passing of the Acts of 1884 was recognized as an imperative necessity.

In the six years which followed the first General Election under the extended franchise, the popular organizations have played an increasingly important part, with the result that considerable alterations have been made in procedure, both before and during an election.

Education. Previous to the contest the local associations undertake a vast amount of work in connection with the political education of the electorate by means of public meetings, the distribution of literature on the questions of the day, and by various other methods of a semi-political, semi-social character, which it would be beyond the purpose of the present book to describe. All this work may be, and often is, done without any candidate being before the constituency, and it cannot therefore be wondered at that those who, in the interests of their party, have devoted time, labour, and money to political work should be more exacting when a candidate for Parliamentary honours appears before them than was formerly the case. They want a champion who is both willing and able to throw himself into the fight with the persistence and industry which go so far to secure a triumph at the poll.

Candidates and Constituencies. On the other hand, a well-organized constituency with good local committees in every polling district offers a much more alluring prospect to a candidate than was the case under a restricted franchise with unlimited expenditure. Then, the party strings were pulled by small and often interested cliques, whose so-called " knowledge of the constituency " was often the merest conjecture ; while the candidate seldom knew what his expenses would be till the election was over and the bills were presented for payment. Now, in spite of defects which are inseparable from all human schemes, a candidate has the means of testing his prospects by the educational work done, and by the information collected through the central organization; and he has the further advantage of being able to fix with certainty the amount of his expenditure.

One or two of the more important points which should receive careful attention prior to an election may perhaps be enumerated with advanvantage. *Prior to Election.*

1. Immediately the new registers can be obtained a complete set of wrappers or envelopes should be addressed, and the canvass books and district registers *prepared in proper street or walking order*.

2. The Polling District Committees should be called together, and each member of a Committee should be allotted a street, road, or group of houses, for which he will thereafter be held responsible.

3. The Polling District Committee should meet at regular intervals, when the register should be checked, and information on the following points reported and marked up :—

　　(a) The death of any voter.
　　(b) The removal of an elector, with the
　　　address to which he has removed.

(c) The name and address of any new-comer, with such particulars as to his politics, and the place from whence he has come, as it may be possible to ascertain.

(d) Additional information as to the politics of electors in the Polling District. *Care should be taken not to mark the registers in this respect unless absolutely positive information can be given, as it is much better in all doubtful cases to rely upon a thorough canvass during the election.*

4. The Chairman or Secretary of the Polling District should ascertain where Committee Rooms for the election may be had, and upon what terms.

It should be remembered that the use as Committee Rooms of premises where refreshment of any kind is ordinarily sold for consumption on the premises, of clubs other than permanent political clubs, and of Public Elementary Schools is prohibited.

5. The Chairman or Secretary should also find out suitable places for holding public meetings, and the terms on which they are available. *There is no legal restriction as to the premises whereon public meetings may be held.*

6. The Polling District Committees should ascertain and report at their meetings the names and addresses of all persons—

(a) Who are willing to lend vehicles or horses on the polling day.

*Horses or vehicles ordinarily let for hire
are not to be used for the conveyance of
voters to the poll.*

(b) Who will *without payment* exhibit
placards or other bills in their windows,
or allow them to be posted on their
premises during the election.

It is beyond doubt desirable that this work
should be done systematically, whether a candidate is before the constituency or not ; but it is
imperative that it should be put in hand
vigorously, when an early dissolution of Parliament is expected and may be announced at
any moment. Of course, it will sometimes
happen in rural districts that Working Committees cannot be formed, but it is generally
possible to find one or two active men who will
render much valuable assistance to the Central
Executive.

In considering the steps which should be taken
by those responsible in case of a Parliamentary
vacancy, it is obvious that the circumstances
under which the vacancy occurs will largely
determine the character of the proceedings.
This is especially the case in the initial
stages. *Parlia-mentary vacancies.*

Elections usually occur from one of the
following causes :—

(a) Resignation (which is accomplished by
applying for the stewardship of the Chil-
tern Hundreds).

(b) Acceptance of an office of profit under the Crown.

(c) Death.

(d) Succession to the Peerage.

(e) Dissolution of Parliament :—

    1. *On the advice of the Cabinet.*

    2. *On the death of the reigning Monarch.*

When a vacancy from any one of these causes is announced or expected, it is the duty of the local Liberal Association to put itself into communication with its candidate without delay. If from any cause no candidate has been adopted, the officers of the Association ought immediately to institute inquiries, with a view to securing, if possible, a local representative. At the same time it would be well for them to invite the co-operation of the central organization of the party in London.

Bye Elections. Bye-elections are now contested with a spirit and determination quite unknown in the days of a limited franchise. The highest organizing talent and the fullest resources of both the great political parties are called into the arena, and all concerned are compelled by the heat of party strife to work with a zeal and energy which ensure that nothing is left undone which by any chance can secure advantage to either side.

It is not contended that the boldest and most skilful agents can win elections against the will of the electors ; but it is generally admitted that in a modern bye-election, especially when the voting strength of a constituency is pretty evenly divided, that party which is best led and best organized is most likely to win. The function, in fact, of skilful agents is to see that no advantage is lost to their party through neglect or bad management.

In a general election it is, of course, impossible that the same forces can be brought into play on either side. The professional agents will then be occupied each in his own constituency, and the sub-districts will perforce be manned, as heretofore, by less practised hands.

A General Election.

Although in bye-elections it is necessary to carry out all the operations described with greater precision, and usually at much higher pressure, than is the case at a general election, it may be taken for granted that good organization always tells, and as many seats are won or lost by small majorities, no pains should be spared, even in a general election, to attain as nearly as possible to perfection in matters of detail. Above all it should never be forgotten by those concerned in electoral work that energy and close attention to the business of the contest rank equally with enthusiasm as winning qualities in all elections.

Necessity for good Organization.

THE CANDIDATE.

Qualifica-
tions of a
Candi-
date. IT is hardly within the scope of a work of this size to deal fully with the various matters affecting the fitness or unfitness of a person in the eyes of the law to represent a constituency in Parliament; but it appears desirable to indicate briefly who are and who are not eligible for election.

There are two essential qualifications which a candidate must fulfil :—

    1. He must be a natural born subject; and

    2. Of the full age of 21 years.

Disquali-
fications
classified. As regards disqualifications, it will be most convenient to follow the classification adopted by Parker, namely :—

    A. Incapacity by reason of infirmity or mental imbecility.

    B. Incapacity by reason of circumstances, character, or conduct.

    C. Incapacity by reason of holding certain offices or positions.

(Election Agent and Returning Officer. Parker, 2nd edition, p. 63.)

The following is a list of persons disqualified in their different classes :—

Class A. Idiots, lunatics, infants, infirm persons (deaf and dumb persons are disqualified, but not those who are blind only), women.

Class B. Aliens, bankrupts, any person reported by an Election Court as guilty of corrupt practices by himself or his agents in a Parliamentary Election ; or if convicted on indictment or information of a corrupt practice at any Parliamentary Election ; or a candidate or other person convicted of corrupt practices at a Municipal Election. A candidate reported by an Election Court to have been personally guilty of illegal practices is disqualified for the particular county or borough for a period of seven years after the date of the report ; or if guilty by his agents, during the Parliament for which the election was held.

Outlaws, traitors, felons, and misdemeanants convicted of fraud or gross breach of trust.

Class C. Priests or deacons of the Church of England, ministers of the Church of Scotland, persons in holy orders in the Church of Rome, contractors for or on account of the public service

Permanent paid officers of a County Council.

Governors and Deputy-Governors of Colonies.

Judges of the High Court of Justice and the Court of Appeal ; the Court of Session and the

Court of Exchequer in Scotland; the High Court of Justice and the Court of Appeal in Ireland; the Court of Bankruptcy and Insolvency in Ireland; the Landed Estates Court, Ireland; the Irish Land Commission; and the County Courts.

A paid Chairman or Deputy-Chairman of the London Quarter Sessions during his term of office.

Stipendiary Magistrates appointed for the Staffordshire Potteries, or Wolverhampton, or for the *Manchester Division*,* or for the Borough of Salford.

A Justice of the Peace or Receiver appointed under the Metropolitan Police Act, 1829; or a Commissioner or Assistant Commissioner of the Metropolitan Police; the Commissioner of the City of London Police; also any Justice of the Peace, Receiver, or person holding office in or under the City of Dublin Police; and the Inspectors, Receivers, and Magistrates of the Irish Constabulary.

Persons holding new offices or places of profit under the Crown created since the 25th October, 1705.

Peers (excepting Irish Peers who have not

---

* No similar disqualification is imposed upon Stipendiary Magistrates appointed for the *Borough* of Manchester, or for Chatham and Sheerness, or under the Stipendiary Magistrates' Act, 1863. Parker, p. 85.

been elected as representative Peers in the House of Lords).

Persons holding pensions from the Crown during pleasure, or for any term of years.*

The Registrar and Deputy-Registrar of Deeds in Middlesex, and every person receiving profit out of the office.

Certain public officers in the Civil Service expressly disqualified.

(For list see Parker, 2nd edition, p. 91.)

The disqualification in the following cases is only partial : —

Returning Officers are ineligible within their own shires or boroughs except that a Sheriff may stand for a borough within his shire *provided the writ is directed to some other Returning Officer.*

Recorders are ineligible for their own boroughs.

A Revising Barrister is not eligible in any place for which he has been appointed for a period of 18 months from the time of his appointment.

It will be the business of the Election Agent to assure himself that the candidate for whom he is acting cannot be objected to on any of the foregoing grounds; and *per contra* he should ascertain whether the opposing candidate is open to valid objection.

* Pensions granted for Civil Services, and pensions under the Diplomatic Salaries, etc., Act, 1869, do not disqualify.

The first matter which claims the attention of a candidate when an election is expected is the appointment of an election agent, unless indeed he intends to act as his own agent. The objections to this alternative are, however, so obvious that it is seldom adopted. The election agent plays so important and responsible a part that very great care should be exercised in his selection.

The election agent's appointment should be signed by the candidate, and should be in the form given below.

APPOINTMENT OF ELECTION AGENT.

Parliamentary Election for the . . . Division of the . . . of . . .
I . . . a Candidate at the above Election, hereby appoint . . . of . . .
to act as my Election Agent from this date until the return and declaration respecting election expenses have been duly made, and I agree to pay the said . . . the sum of £ . . . for his services as such Election Agent. . . .   Dated this . . . day of . . . 189 .   (Signed)

From the moment the election agent is appointed the candidate's responsibility for the numerous details of the election practically ceases, and is transferred to the agent. The candidate should refer all matters relating to the conduct and management of the election to his agent. He may also find it desirable to consult his agent from time to time upon questions of policy, but of course such questions, strictly speaking, are no concern of the election agent, except in so far as they affect the prospect of a successful termination of the contest.

On or before the day of election (*i.e.*, of nomination) the candidate is required to send to the returning officer notice of the appointment of his election agent, or, in case he elects to be his own agent, notice of such intention. A form for this purpose is here suggested.

Notice to Returning Officer of Appointment of Election Agent.

DECLARATION TO THE RETURNING OFFICER OF NAME AND ADDRESS OF ELECTION AGENT.

Parliamentary Election for the . . . Division of the . . . of . . . I . . . a Candidate at the above-named Election, do hereby give you notice that my Election Agent is . . . of . . . and that the address of his office, to which all notices, etc., with regard to the said Election may be sent, is . . .   Dated this . . . day of . . . 189 .   (Signed)
    To the Returning Officer

Having appointed his election agent, and being thus assured that the detail business and organization will proceed forthwith, the next matter which will occupy the candidate's attention is the preparation of his address to the electors. Too much attention cannot be given to this subject. The convictions of the candidate upon matters of public policy should be stated in the briefest form compatible with plain and vigorous expression. With reference to subjects having a peculiar interest to the bulk of the electorate in the constituency he seeks to represent, or having an entirely local significance, the candidate would do well to seek the advice of his election agent and of the leading men of his party in the locality. No delay, except such as is demanded by decency in case of death, should be permitted in getting the candidate's address written out and printed. A keen interest is generally taken by the electors

Address to the Electors.

in political contests, and the candidate who delays issuing his address may suffer therefrom to an irreparable extent.

Personal Expenses. There is one other matter which the candidate should attend to with some care, namely, the record of his personal expenses. These will include his own travelling and hotel expenses, and, within reasonable limits, the entertainment of friends who come at their own cost to assist in the election. There must not, however, be the slightest doubt as to the *bonâ-fides* of the candidate's friends. They must not be paid agents either of the candidate or of any Association acting in his interests, but must be voluntary helpers in the strictest sense. For example, a candidate may entertain for the night at an hotel (or at his own house) any Member of Parliament or other friend who may come to speak in support of his candidature. Any person may, of course, assist in this way at an election at his own cost.

The candidate's personal expenses are altogether independent of the ordinary election expenses, and need not be taken into account in connection with the maximum expenditure allowed under the Corrupt Practices Act, 1883. They are not limited to any particular amount; and up to £100 it would appear that the candidate is not called upon to render any detailed account. It would, however, be well for the candidate to keep a memorandum of his expenses for his private use and information. If the candidate's personal expenses exceed £100, the excess above such £100 must be paid by the election agent, and a detailed account sent with the return of election expenses to the returning officer.

The candidate must within fourteen days after the date of the election inform his election agent in writing of the total amount of his personal expenses as paid by himself.

The candidate is required to make a statutory declaration respecting the election expenses. It is best that this should accompany the return sent in by the election agent ; but it may be forwarded any time within seven days of the lodging of such return, or, if the candidate is then abroad, within fourteen days after his return to the United Kingdom (C. P. A., 1883, Sec. 33). *Candidate to make declaration as to election expenses.*

It is of the greatest importance that the requirements of this section should be fulfilled, as the member cannot sit or vote in Parliament unless the return and declarations are lodged within the specified time. Certain provision is made under Section 34 of the Act for relief in case of failure to comply with the requirements of the Act; but as it is only in very rare cases that such failure can be deemed excusable, no candidate or agent should rely upon this provision.

The following is the form of declaration by a candidate :—

DECLARATION AS TO EXPENSES BY CANDIDATE.

Parliamentary Election for the . . . of . . . I . . . having been a candidate at the election for the county [or borough] of . . . on the . . . day of . . . do hereby solemnly and sincerely declare that I have examined the return of election expenses [about to be] transmitted by my election agent [*or if the candidate is his own election agent,* " by me "] to the returning officer at the said election, a copy of which is now shown to me and marked . . . and to the best of my knowledge and belief that return is correct. And I further solemnly and sincerely declare that, except as appears from that return, I have not, and to the best of my knowledge and belief no person, nor any club, society, or association, has, on my behalf, made any payment, or given, promised, or offered any reward, office, employment, or valuable consideration, or incurred any liability on account of or in respect of the conduct or management of the said election. And I further solemnly and sincerely declare that I have paid to my election agent [*if the candidate is also his own election agent, leave out* " to my election agent "] the sum of . . . pounds and no more for the purpose of the said election, and that, except as specified in the said return, no money, security, or equivalent for money has to my knowledge or belief been paid, advanced, given, or deposited by anyone to or in the hands of my election agent [*or if the candidate is his own election agent,* " myself "] or any other person for the purpose of defraying any expenses incurred on my behalf on account of or in respect of the conduct or management of the said election. And I further solemnly and sincerely declare that I will not, except so far as I may be permitted by law, at any future time make or be party to the making or giving of any payment, reward, office, employment, or valuable consideration for the purpose of defraying any such expenses as last mentioned, or provide or te party to the providing of any money, security, or equivalent for money for the purpose of defraying any such expenses. Signature of declarant . . . Signed and declared by the above-named declarant on the . . . day of . . . before me. (Signed) . . . Justice of the Peace for . . .

When Candidate is abroad. It sometimes happens that a candidate, or some person whom it is considered desirable to nominate as a candidate, is abroad at the time a vacancy occurs, and cannot be communicated with before the date fixed for the election. In such a case he may be nominated in the ordinary way, but it is provided that " if he is so nominated or declared as a candidate without his consent, nothing in this Act shall be construed to impose any liability upon such person, unless he has afterwards given his assent to such nomination or declaration or has been elected " (C. P. A., Sec. 63).   If the candidate should not approve the nomination, the persons signing his nomination paper would be liable for the Returning Officer's charges (38 and 39 Vict., c. 84, Sec. 2).   If a candidate is going abroad and a dissolution or election is expected to take place during his absence, it is desirable that he should leave, in the hands of some responsible person, a written authority for his nomination.

THE ELECTION AGENT.

Personal qualifications. UNDER the conditions created by the Corrupt Practices Act, 1883, the election agent occupies a position of the gravest responsibility. It is not sufficient that he should have a thorough knowledge of election law, but he must be a man of ability and character; he must combine tact with firmness; he ought to have a thorough knowledge of current politics, and should be intimately acquainted with the practical details of electoral work. Nothing can legally be done without his sanction, and where large and enthusiastic committees exist, there is great danger of conflict and confusion, unless the agent is a man of ability and even temper. He will constantly be urged by irresponsible and over-zealous partisans to resort to questionable, if not absolutely illegal, methods; and he must, therefore, be a man possessing the necessary firmness of character, not only to resist such importunities, but to prevent others from resorting to improper practices. To the qualities already named should be added the very desirable ones of energy and force of character sufficient to make his personal influence effective in con-

nection with the minutest details of the work
and the smallest actions of .his many helpers.
It is not, of course, contended that the most
perfect election agent can ensure victory under
all conditions ; but in a closely-contested election a good agent may win, while an indifferent
or inexperienced man would most probably lose.

There are certain legal requirements and Legal
restrictions which must be observed in the case ments. require-
of the election agent, and which may be set
forth here.

1. A paid election agent cannot vote in the
county or borough where the election in
which he is acting is being held.

2. No person who has, within seven years,
previously been declared by any competent tribunal guilty of any corrupt practice can be engaged as election agent. If
such a person were appointed by the
candidate personally, with a knowledge
of such disqualification, the election of
the latter would be voided.

3. On or before the nomination day the
name and address of the election agent
must be declared in writing to the returning officer. At the same time the address
of an office where claims, notices, and
other documents may be sent, and which
must be within the borough or county in
which the election is proceeding (or
within any county of a city or town

adjoining thereto), must be declared to the returning officer.

Central Committee room. In beginning the business of the election, the election agent should establish himself in a conveniently situated central committee-room; and it is of importance that this central committee-room in counties should be in the town which is best adapted as a centre for working the election, regard being had, amongst other important matters, to geographical considerations, railway, postal, and telegraphic communications, etc. It too often happens that the election is worked from a central office in some out-of-the-way corner of a constituency, whence it is impossible for a proper supervision to be exercised, and with which it is difficult for the remoter parts of the division to maintain communication.

Election Agent's duty is superintendence. The election agent should take care not to burden himself with any detail work that he can avoid. There are certain matters, such as the organization of committees; the hiring of committee-rooms and halls for public meetings; the appointment of sub-agents, clerks, messengers, and personation agents; the preparation and examination of nomination papers; the issuing of orders for printing, etc.; and watching the expenditure, for which he must in the main be responsible; but while acquainting himself minutely with everything that is going on in the election, he should keep his mind clear for the general superintendence of the work, and should not himself undertake the sole responsibility for any one branch of it.

Where the party organization has been conducted in the most perfect manner, the local political association will have made many preparations for an election, and the election agent will simply have to take over the work which has been done.

In such a case there will be ready :—

> 1. Envelopes addressed to every elector on the Parliamentary register.

> By the new Post Office regulation which came into force on the 1st January, 1892, envelopes, if left open for inspection by the officials, may be used instead of halfpenny wrappers. Care should be taken that the register number of each elector is put on the envelope, as this will be found a great convenience when identifying the returned letters.

> 2. Polling district registers, containing, in street order, the name, address, and register number of every elector in each polling district.

> 3. Canvass books, also made out in street order, each book having about twenty names in it.

> 4. Lists of voluntary helpers in each polling district.

> 5. A record of the names and addresses of persons in each polling district who are willing to let or lend committee-rooms, and also of friends who will lend vehicles on the polling day.

> 6. There should also be a list of the places

where public meetings may be held, with an estimate of the number of persons who can be accommodated.

Where these things are not already prepared the election agent must at once put them in hand. He will require a large staff to get the envelopes addressed, but very frequently a number of voluntary helpers can be found. Ladies' aid is especially valuable at this stage, and they are usually eager to undertake the work.

Matters needing immediate attention:—
1. Preparation of Canvass Books, &c. The canvass books and district registers should be prepared under the supervision of the election agent, or some person deputed by him. Where the register is in street order this will be a comparatively simple matter, but where the lists are made out in alphabetical order great care must be exercised. The simplest plan is to address a set of envelopes, and have them sorted in proper order by persons who know the streets or roads intimately. The district registers and canvass books can then be written up from these. Specimen headings of district registers and canvass books supplied by the publishers of this book are given below.

DISTRICT REGISTER.

Street No.	Name of Voter.	Register No.	For.	Against.	Favourable.	Doubtful.	Dead.	Removed.	Time Vehicle Wanted.	Remarks.

CANVASS BOOK.

House No.	Name of Voter.	Register No.	For.	Against.	Favourable.	Doubtful.	Dead.	Removed.	Remarks.

Simultaneously with this work the election agent should put in hand the candidate's address to the electors. It is usually of the greatest importance that this address should be issued early, and it is the election agent's duty to see that it is not delayed. *2. Printing and circulation of Candidate's Address.*

A sufficient number of copies of the election address should be printed to permit of one being forwarded by post to every elector, and for a few to be sent to each committee-room. Thus, in a constituency of 10,000 electors, it will be well to have at least 12,500 copies struck off at the outset. It is usual also to print a number of large posters. This is, however, an expensive business, and it is very doubtful whether the advantage of the practice is in any way commensurate with the cost.

Other matters needing the immediate attention of the election agent are :— *3. Appointment of Sub-agents, &c.*

 (1) The appointment of sub-agents;

 (2) The appointment of clerks and messengers;

 (3) The grouping of polling districts for working purposes;

(4) The securing of suitable committee-
    rooms ; and

(5) The drawing up of a scheme of public
    meetings to be held during the contest.

These matters are dealt with in detail under
separate headings ; but the election agent should
note in regard to the appointment of sub-agents,
clerks, and messengers, that while these appointments need not necessarily be in writing it is
very desirable that a memorandum setting forth
the terms of the appointment should be signed
by each party. The following simple form is
suggested :—

APPOINTMENT OF SUB-AGENT.

I . . . of . . . hereby accept an engagement as Sub-Agent on the terms set forth in the ap-pointment now handed to me by . . . Fee : . . . inclusive of all ex-penses other than election ex-penses authorized by me. Dated his . . . day of . . . 189 . (Signed) . . .

APPOINTMENT OF SUB-AGENT.

To . . . of . . . I . . . Election Agent for . . . a Candidate at the Parliamentary Election now being held in the . . . Division of the County of . . . hereby appoint you to act as my Sub-Agent for the Poll-ing District of . . . from the present date till the declaration of the poll ; and I agree to pay you the sum of £ . . . as a fee to include all expenses other than election expenses autho-rized by me. Dated this . . . day of . . . 189 . (Signed) . . .

One sub-agent, and no more, may be appointed
to act within each polling district. The election
agent should, however, bear in mind that each
sub-agent is a deputy election agent, and that
any act, or default, of such deputy-agent has
almost invariably the same effect as any act, or
default, of the election agent. Apart, therefore,
from the question of expense, it is desirable to
limit the number of sub-agents as far as is con-

sistent with a due regard to the efficient working of the election. One sub-agent may generally, with advantage, be given the oversight of two or more polling districts.

The election agent must, one clear day before the polling, declare in writing the name and address of every sub-agent to the returning officer, and at the same time he should state the address of the offices within their respective polling districts, to which notices, writs, or other documents may be sent to such sub-agents.

Name and Address of Sub-agent to be declared to Returning Officer.

It is suggested that the election agent should deliver to every sub-agent, with his appointment, the following instructions :—

INSTRUCTIONS TO SUB-AGENTS.

1.—Your duties within your own district are similar to those of the Election Agent; and you are subject to the same disabilities. In the event of your committing any act infringing the law or being in default in any particular, your act of default will have the same effect as if committed by the Election Agent, and you are subject to the same penalties.

2.—You are hereby authorized to incur expenditure in respect of petty expenses in connection with the Election to an amount not exceeding £... On no account must you exceed this sum without receiving a further authority in writing from me.

3.—The number of Polling Districts under your control is ...

4.—The number of Committee Rooms for which payment may be made is limited to ... and you must not engage more. If necessary you may accept the loan of other Committee Rooms, but you must make it clear to the lender that neither during the Election nor afterwards will any payment be made for the same.

5.—No Committee Room may be hired or used " in any premises licensed for the sale, wholesale or retail, of intoxicating liquors, nor in any premises where any intoxicating liquor is sold or supplied to members of a club, society, or association other than a permanent political club, nor in any premises where the refreshments are sold for consumption on the premises."—C. P. A., s. 20.

You will, therefore, be careful to avoid engaging Committee Rooms in public-houses, brewers' or wine merchants' premises, coffee or eating houses, confectioners' shops where refreshments are consumed on the premises, grocers' shops with licenses attached, &c., &c.

Do not engage rooms in the premises of any club without first consulting me, and it will be advisable not to contemplate using such rooms until every other alternative has been exhausted.

6.—You will engage your own clerks, messengers, and personation agents. The number of clerks and messengers that you may employ is limited to . . . Do not engage the full number of clerks or messengers unless it be absolutely necessary; and it is suggested that at least one of the messengers should be a good bicycle rider.

The clerks you may pay at a rate not exceeding *£ : : per week, and the messengers £ : : per week.

7.—One polling or personation agent is allowed for each Polling Station, and you should endeavour to secure the services of gentlemen who are well acquainted with and well known to the electors in the district for which they will act. No doubt you will be able to obtain voluntary help in this matter; but in case you have to pay any person, the amount offered should not exceed £1 for the day.

8.—It is important that you should devote particular attention to the organization of efficient local committees; and also that you should institute a thorough canvass under your constant personal supervision.

You will also arrange a sufficient number of public meetings within your districts, and inform me of your requirements as regards speakers at the earliest possible moment.

9.—All printing, except that necessary for advertising meetings within the Polling Districts under your control, will be done through the Central Office; and the amount you are authorized to spend must be understood to cover the cost of any printing necessary in connection with your meetings. Any extra printing that you may require done you should communicate with me about. You will bear in mind that every "bill, placard, or poster" must bear upon its face the name and address of the printer and publisher.

10.—It is important to remember that no payment, or promise of payment, may be made on account of—

    (a) The conveyance of voters to or from the poll;

    (b) For bands of music, torches, flags, banners, cockades, ribbons, or other marks of distinction;

    (c) To any elector for the exhibition of bills, addresses, or notices, unless such elector is a bill-poster or advertising agent, and receives payment in the ordinary course of his business.

11.—No cockade, ribbon, or other mark of distinction may be given to, or provided for, any voter or inhabitant.

12.—Every appointment, and all agreements for the hire of rooms for public meetings, committee-rooms, &c., must be made by yourself. If made by any other person the appointment or contract would be illegal.

13.—You will make all necessary arrangements for the work on the polling day within your districts.

---

* The rate of pay will vary so greatly according to the district and the capabilities of the persons employed that it is impossible to fix a scale applicable to all cases; but it is suggested that as a general rule £2 per week for clerks and 30s. for messengers would be a reasonable limit.

14.—You will receive notice of all Voters who have removed from other Polling Districts into the districts in your charge; and *you will be responsible for sending such Voters to the place where they are to Poll and taking them back to their homes.*

You will not be responsible for fetching Voters who have removed from your districts to others, except in such cases as may be agreed upon.

15.—At the close of the Poll you will be expected to collect and forward to me, at the Central Committee Room, without delay, all books, papers, notices, registers, lists, and other documents relating to the election.

16.—Also, it will be necessary for you to get in and pay all claims against you in respect of the election within your district. This should be done within as short a time as possible, but all claims must be sent in within fourteen days of the date of the declaration of the result of the Election, or they cannot be recognized.

Any payment amounting to 40s. or over you must vouch for by a bill stating the particulars of the goods supplied, and receipted by the person paid.

17.—If you dispute any claim a full statement of the reasons for doing so must be sent to me by you, together with the particulars of the claim and the name and address of the person making it.

18.—It will be necessary for you to send to me, within twenty-eight days after the declaration of the Poll, a full statement of all accounts paid by you, together with the necessary vouchers.

(Signed) . . . Election Agent.

As soon as the sub-agents' appointments have been completed, the election agent should have printed, and a copy sent to every district committee-room, a list giving the sub-agents' names and addresses, the polling districts under their control, and the villages or parishes in their polling districts. **List of Sub-agents.**

The following is suggested as a convenient form :—

Polling District.	Villages or Parishes.	No. of Voters on Register.	Sub-Agent.	Address.
Bere Regis.	Bere Regis. Winterbourne.	191 100	G. E. H.	15, Market Place, Bere Regis.

This list is necessary to enable sub-agents to communicate with each other, and it is also extremely useful to the election agent himself, and to the members of the Election Committee.

The number of paid clerks and messengers allowed is as follows :—

For the central committee-room one clerk and one messenger; or if the number of electors in the Division exceeds 5,000, one clerk and one messenger for every complete 5,000 or fraction of 5,000, that is to say,—if the number of electors is 5,000, one clerk and one messenger; if the number of electors is 10,000, two clerks and two messengers; if the number of electors is 10,001, three clerks and three messengers, and so on for each 5,000.

For each polling district, one clerk and one messenger; or where the number of electors in the polling district exceeds 500, one clerk and one messenger for each complete 500 or fraction of 500, that is to say,—if the number of electors in the polling district is 500, one clerk and one messenger; if the number of electors in the polling district is 1,000, two clerks and two messengers; if the number of electors in the polling district is 1,001, three clerks and three messengers. Provided the full number is not exceeded clerks and messengers may be employed in any polling district where their services are required.

The election agent by himself or his sub-agent must appoint every polling agent, clerk, or messenger. (C. P. A., Sec. 27, Sub-Sec. 1.)

The same provision applies to the hiring of committee-rooms.

As to the manner in which the election agent should organize his own staff of clerks it is suggested that he should proceed as follows :—

Appoint one clerk, whose sole duty it shall be to assist him with the correspondence, to write out orders to printers and others, *though these should always be signed by the agent,* and to keep an account of the expenditure incurred. This account should be made up daily under the different heads given in the Act, and should be examined by the election agent.

In elections where meetings play an important part, it is also well to appoint a competent man to superintend the arrangements throughout the constituency. His duty would be—

(*a*) To conduct the correspondence with the speakers on behalf of the election agent ;

(*b*) To advise the local managers when to arrange meetings ;

(*c*) To draft handbills and posters and to get them printed and sent to the different districts for circulation, excepting of course when it is arranged that the sub-agent is to get his own bills printed ;

(*d*) To see that speakers coming from a distance are met at the station and conveyed to the place where the meeting is to be held ;

(e) That, when desired, accommodation
and refreshment are provided for such
speakers ; and, generally,

(f) To see that the arrangements for meetings are complete and satisfactory to all
concerned.

A clerk will also be required to deal with removals, and another should be appointed to
arrange for vehicles on the polling day, and, with
an assistant, to distribute leaflets and other
literature to the different polling districts.

These with two messengers will usually be
found sufficient for the central office.

Persona-
tion and
Counting
Agents.
Personation agents and counting agents should
be arranged for either by the election agent or his
sub-agents. It is desirable, generally speaking,
that these appointments should be made in
writing by the election agent himself.

Forms of appointment and of notice to the
returning officer are given on p. 32.

Notice must be given by the election agent
to the returning officer of the names and
addresses of the personation agents appointed.
If this is not done the returning officer may
refuse to admit any agent to the polling station.
There is no provision in the Act that this notice
shall be delivered before the opening of the poll ;
but it is, for obvious reasons, convenient to do so.
One personation agent for each polling station
and no more may be engaged for payment.

As regards agents to attend the counting of

the votes, they must, if employed for payment, be appointed by the election agent or his sub-agents; and as the number allowed in the counting room is regulated by the returning officer, the election agent should always reserve to himself the right of making these appointments. The agents, in so far as paid agents are employed, must be chosen from amongst the sub-agents, polling agents, clerks, or messengers, since there is no provision in the Corrupt Practices Act for payment of counting agents as distinct officials. In the case of counting agents acting gratuitously the candidate may make the appointments.

In any case the election agent should consult the returning officer or his deputy with regard to the number of counting agents who will be admitted; and the appointments must be made and notice of such appointments given to the returning officer at least one clear day before the opening of the poll. For example, if the poll be fixed for the 3rd of the month notice of the appointments must reach the returning officer on the 1st.

The election agent should take care that the personation and counting agents make the necessary declaration of secrecy before a magistrate. Any magistrate, whether acting within the county or not, may attest the declaration.

Forms of appointment and of notice to the

returning officer follow.   The declaration in both cases is the same.

APPOINTMENT OF POLLING OR PERSONATION AGENT.

Parliamentary Election for the . . . Division of the . . . of . . . To . . . of . . . You are hereby appointed as an Agent on behalf of . . . a Candidate in the above Election, to detect personation, and you are required to attend at Polling Station No. . . . on . . . the . . . day of . . . from 8 a.m. to 8 p.m. . . . (Signed) . . . Agent.

Before proceeding to the Polling Station you must make the following declaration before a Justice of the Peace.

DECLARATION.

I solemnly promise and declare that I will not at this Election for the . . . Division of the . . . of . . . do anything forbidden by Section 4 of the Ballot Act, 1872, which has been read to me . . . (Signed) . . .

This declaration was made before me, a Justice of the Peace for the . . . of . . . this . . . day of . . . 189 . . . (Signed) . . .

NOTICE TO BE GIVEN TO THE RETURNING OFFICER OF NAMES AND ADDRESSES OF POLLING OR PERSONATION AGENTS.

Parliamentary Election for the . . . Division of the . . . of . . . I . . . being the Election Agent for . . . a Candidate at the above Election, do hereby give you notice that I have appointed the persons whose names and addresses here follow to attend at the Polling Stations indicated opposite their names and to act on behalf of the said Candidate as Agents to detect Personation.

Name.	Address.	To attend at Polling Station.

NOTICE TO BE GIVEN TO THE RETURNING OFFICER OF NAMES AND ADDRESSES OF AGENTS APPOINTED TO ATTEND THE COUNTING.

Parliamentary Election for the . . . Division of the . . . of . . . I . . . being the Election Agent for . . . a Candidate at the above Election, do hereby give you notice that the persons whose names here follow have been appointed as Agents to attend the Counting on behalf of the said candidate.

Name.	Address.

The election agent must see that nomination Nomination Papers. papers are filled up on behalf of the candidate he represents. Further information on this point will be found on p. 80.

The election agent should ascertain at the Polling Cards. earliest possible moment what arrangements the returning officer intends to make for the taking of the poll; and as soon as he knows where the polling stations are to be, he must, with the utmost possible despatch, prepare the voters' instruction card, or polling card, as it is usually called. Indeed, it will be advisable to have this card set up beforehand, in readiness for the insertion of the address of the polling place. The instructions on the card should be *brief*, and care must be taken in wording it that no statement is made which will mislead the voter, or which could be construed as an infringement of the laws protecting electors.

The form given below would be suitable :—

> . . . Parliamentary Election, 189 . Mr. . . . begs to inform you that the poll will take place on* . . . from eight o'clock in the morning till eight in the evening. You are thus described on the Register.
>
> No. . . . Name . . .
> You must vote at . . .

On the reverse side :—

> Your attention is respectfully requested to the following points :—
> On entering the polling station you will receive from the presiding officer a ballot-paper; please fill it up by making a distinct X in the space opposite the name of . . . ; thus —

1.	A.	X
2.	B.		

* State the day of the week and date.

D

*Make no other mark than the X, as shown above, or your vote will be
lost to Mr. . . .*

When you have marked the paper, fold it up. so that no one can
see for whom you have voted, *show the official mark on the back
to the presiding officer,* and then put the paper in the ballot-box.

Poll as early as possible.

The ballot is absolutely secret, and you need not tell anyone how
you have voted.

In printing these cards the name of the candidate for whom it is desired that the elector
should vote is sometimes shown in larger type
than that of his opponent. It is submitted that
this is a mistake, and is calculated to mislead
some voters, inasmuch as on the ballot-paper
itself both names are printed the same size.
This is a small point, but it is well worthy of
consideration.

It is also submitted that it is undesirable to
ask electors to report at the committee-room
after they have voted. The election agent's
arrangements should enable him to ascertain
when an elector has been to the poll without
subjecting him to inconvenience, and possibly to
injury, through his visit to the committee-room.
Occasionally the polling instructions are printed
on the back of ordinary post-cards. This expedient, of course, lessens the expense; but it
prevents the enclosure of leaflets or other literature bearing on the election, and is to this extent
less effective.

Distribu-
tion of
Polling
Cards.

In a perfectly organized constituency it will
probably be considered desirable to distribute
the poll cards through the local committees.
The advantage of this plan is that it enables the

canvassers to have a last word with the electors
on the eve of the poll. In such cases it is absolutely necessary that the cards should be in the
hands of the sub-agents at least four days before
the opening of the poll, and more time should
be given, if possible.

Generally, however, the cards are sent out by
post, and, under these circumstances, the sub-
agents (if they send them out) should have the
cards early enough to enable them to be despatched not less than two days before the poll.
It may even be necessary, in some districts, that
the cards should be posted earlier than this, in
order to secure their delivery in due time. It is
obvious that there are disadvantages in sending
out the cards too early, and the agents should
take care that no error is made on either side.

Arrangements should be made with the local
postmaster to receive the cards at a time agreed
upon.

Care should be taken that the envelopes are
prepared in readiness, and that all needful cor-
rection of addresses is made before posting the
poll cards.

It has become a practice for a portrait of the
candidate to be circulated amongst the electors,
and there is no doubt that this is sometimes an
effective electioneering move ; but, if done at all,
it is essential that the workmanship should be
the best obtainable. The difference of cost between a bad portrait and a good one is so trifling

Portrait of the Candidate.

that it is not worth while to send out a mere smudge or caricature. The back of the portrait card, which should be of the cabinet size, may be utilized to give a short account of the measures or policy supported by the candidate; or it may be made to serve the purpose of a poll card.

Day of Poll. Before the polling day the election agent must issue notices to all his principal officials instructing them as to their duties on the polling day and afterwards.

The election agent should make the declaration of secrecy, and should see that the candidate and all other persons of whom it is required do the same.

It will be necessary also that the election agent should arrange for the candidate to make a tour of the constituency, or as much of it as he can cover, on the polling day. The committee-rooms and polling stations should be visited. A carriage, relays of horses, and other matters must be duly arranged for; a time-table should be drawn up and as far as possible adhered to. Notice should be given to the sub-agents of the time at which they may expect the candidate to arrive.

The election agent's movements on the polling day will depend to a great extent upon circumstances. If he has a competent man not otherwise occupied whom he can leave in charge of the central committee-room, it will probably be desirable that he should himself visit all his committee-rooms. He will thus be able to assure himself that every man is at his post and that all is in good order; or on the other hand he may be able to remedy defects, supply omissions, or give advice and assistance on the spot in matters of difficulty.

On no account, however, should he leave the central committee-room unless he can place some qualified substitute in charge; and under any circumstances he should leave at the central rooms an address or addresses to which communications may be sent in case of need.

At the close of the poll he should require from his sub-agents a full report as to the number of electors polled in each district.

The election agent should attend the counting of the votes, and should be in time to see the boxes opened and the ballot papers verified.

ELECTION EXPENSES.

IN making his arrangements for the contest the election agent will of necessity be guided by the amount of money placed at his disposal by the candidate ; and in any case he is, of course, limited absolutely to the maximum scale allowed under the Corrupt Practices Act. Many changes have taken place since the passing of this Act. The Redistribution Act of 1885 made sweeping changes as regards area, and the increase and shifting of population have largely altered in many constituencies the conditions then created. It might be thought that a maximum expenditure designed to meet the case of half a county would be beyond the requirements of a Division considerably less in size; but two important points must be borne in mind, namely (1), that the basis of the calculations in the Corrupt Practices Act is the electorate of the district dealt with, and (2) that before the Redistribution Act it was usual to arrange joint candidatures, when the maximum expenditure was increased by one-half. At the present time it may therefore be considered that the maximum scale is not on the average in excess of the amount necessary for efficiently working an election.

In considering what items of expenditure incurred in preparation for a contest he must adopt and account for as part of his election expenses, the election agent must decide whether such expenditure has reference to the "conduct or management of the election" (C. P. A., Sec. 8). Expenditure before Election which must be adopted by Election Agent.

There are many instances in which it will be found very difficult to decide what should be included, and it is, of course, impossible to offer suggestions here which would cover every conceivable case. I am, however, permitted to quote counsel's opinion upon the following points:—

"The Act, unfortunately, does not define what is meant by the 'conduct or management' of an election, but it was decided by Day and Field, J.J., in the Kennington case that those words do not refer to registration expenses. It was pointed out in the judgment in that case that although registration expenses *are incurred on account of an expected election, yet they are no part of the expense of conducting or managing the election itself."* The words italicised appear to afford guidance as to the principle which must govern an election agent's decision in other matters than registration expenses. It would follow therefrom that any expense "incurred on account of an expected election," and yet forming no part of the necessary prepara- Registration Expenses.

tions for the "conduct or management" of the election, may be excluded from the return of election expenses. On the other hand, all work done before the election, which work, or the outcome of it, the election agent takes under his own control for the purposes of the election, must, of course, be paid for by him and included in his return.

Public Meetings and Literature. The question of how far the cost of public meetings and of the distribution of literature, prior to an election, form part of the "conduct or management of the election" is admittedly more difficult. There is no definite authority on the point. Counsel says—

"It was decided in the Kennington case that the cost of a newspaper, which had been started by the candidate substantially for the purpose of supporting his candidature, need not be returned as part of his expenses, and if the candidate is at liberty to prepare the voters for an election by means of newspapers, it might fairly be argued that he is at liberty to do so by means of public meetings and leaflets. But there is this important difference between the cost of registration or of starting newspapers and the cost of meetings and leaflets, viz., that the Act makes no mention of the former, while it expressly includes the latter expense (at all events during the actual period of the election) in the permitted maximum of expenditure. Public meetings and leaflets are, therefore, part of the

'conduct or management' of an election, and
the Act says if money is expended in respect of
the 'conduct or management' of an election,
whether before, during, or after such election, it
should be included in the return. It must not,
however, be inferred from this that *all* public
meetings and leaflets, prior to an election, are
part of its 'conduct or management,' simply
because they form part of the candidate's
political propaganda. To educate the voters
in anticipation of an election is one thing; to
'conduct or manage' the actual election itself is
another. The words 'conduct or management'
are limited to the 'election,' and *apply only to
the period of the election*, but the candidate must
not evade the Act by defraying the expenses *of
that period* BEFORE *the period itself begins*, nor
after it is over. The object of the words 'before,
during, or after an election' is only to prevent
evasion, and to bring within the scope of the
Act all payments which, but for the Act, would
be made during the actual period of the election
(*i.e.*, after the issue of the writ.)" . . . "Thus
. . . if a candidate held *all*, or practically all his
public meetings before the seat was actually
vacant, in order to save that expense afterwards,
and thereby enable himself to devote the maximum expenditure to other matters, the judges
would consider that he was evading the Act, and
that he had paid *before* the election an expense
which ordinarily and properly *belonged to the*

period of the election. But money spent on the political education of voters, whether by the candidate or anybody else, before the legal election begins, is, in my opinion, outside the scope of the Act."

Another point which may assist candidates and election agents to determine what expenditure should be adopt ed is the definition in Section 63 of what constitutes a candidate. A " candidate at an election " is defined to be one who is nominated as candidate or declared to be such after the seat is vacant. Counsel's opinion is that—

" For practical purposes, therefore, the period of the vacancy may be treated as the period of the election."

The election agent should, at the outset, make an approximate calculation of the amount that he can afford to spend under each heading named in the form contained in Schedule II. of the Corrupt Practices Act.

Maximum Scale. Section 8 of the Corrupt Practices Act lays down the rule that —

> "*No sum shall be paid and no expense shall be incurred by a candidate at an election, or his election agent, whether before, during, or after an election, on account of or in respect of the conduct or management of such election, in excess of any maximum amount in that behalf specified in the first schedule to this Act.*"

Any candidate or agent who knowingly acts in contravention of this section will be guilty of an illegal practice.

The maximum scale for England and Scotland is as shown in the following table :—

IN A COUNTY.

Constituency.	For one Candidate.
Not exceeding—	
2,000 electors.	£650
3,000 ,,	£710
4,000 ,,	£770
5,000 ,,	£830
6,000 ,,	£890
7,000 ,,	£950
8,000 ,,	£1,010
9,000 ,,	£1,070
10,000 ,,	£1,130
11,000 ,,	£1,190
12,000 ,,	£1,250
13,000 ,,	£1,310
14,000 ,,	£1,370
15,000 ,,	£1,430

And so on, adding £60 for every complete 1,000 electors.

The following three heads of expenditure are not included in the maximum scale, and expenses falling under them may be incurred in addition to the maximum:— *Expenditure not included in maximum.*

1. Returning officer's charges.
2. Personal expenses of the candidate.
3. Expenses of conveying voters by sea in certain excepted cases.

As regards the personal expenses of the candidate a misapprehension is sometimes found to exist with reference to the meaning of Sub-Section 1, Section 31 of the Corrupt Practices Act. *Personal Expenses.*

It may be desirable, therefore, to quote the Sub-Section :—

*" The candidate at an election may pay any
personal expenses incurred by him on
account of, or in connection with, or incidental to such election to an amount not
exceeding one hundred pounds, but any
further personal expenses so incurred by
him shall be paid by his election agent."*

Part IV. of Schedule I, C. P. A., 1883, expressly states that the maximum excludes "personal expenses;" and the form of return of
election expenses prescribed for the use of the
election agent by Schedule II. contains the following headings :—

Personal expenses of the said C. D., paid by himself.

      ,,   ,,   ,,   paid by me.

These provisions are held to indicate clearly
that the intention of Parliament was to prevent
any abuse arising in connection with the personal
expenditure of candidates, and not to limit
legitimate outlay under this heading.

Personal expenses have been defined as "all
the money he spends in travelling to, from, and
about the constituency, and the cost of his board
and lodging there, together with payments for
food, comforts or luxuries, which can be fairly
included in the cost of living, whether bought in
the constituency or elsewhere, if consumed in
the constituency."

A sugges-
tion for an
estimate.
It is, of course, impossible to lay down any
absolute rule on the subject, but it may be useful
to indicate the amounts which, in practical ex-

perience, have been found sufficient to cover each class of expenditure in a county constituency with 10,500 electors on the register, the maximum allowed being £1,190, and the contest extending over a period of three weeks.

It should be noted that the number of electors is to be taken according to the enumeration in the register, *i.e.*, the duplicate entries need not be deducted in calculating the maximum.

Election agent	£150
Sub-agents	157
Polling agents	20
Clerks	150
Messengers	68
Printing ...	180
Advertising	47
Stationery	20
Postage	92
Telegrams	17
Hire of rooms for public meetings...	78
,, ,, for committee-rooms	24
Miscellaneous	179

(Expenditure under this head is absolutely limited to an amount not exceeding £200).

Having made his estimate, always allowing a good margin to meet contingencies, the agent should exercise the strictest control over the orders given and do his best to keep the amounts within the limit he has allowed himself. Sub-agents should be required to render statements from time to time of the expenses they *Strict control necessary.*

have incurred in their districts, and in no case should they be allowed to exceed the sum they have been authorized to expend, unless a further authority is given them in writing. All orders issued from the central committee-room should be signed by the election agent, and invoices of all goods delivered should be insisted upon, and the amounts of the same entered under their proper heading on the expenses sheet each day. In this way only can the agent see how his expenditure is progressing and control it. Further, this plan will immensely simplify the task of preparing the final return to be made to the returning officer.

Receipts to be taken. When payments made, or claims for payment, amount to 40s. or upwards, the bill must state particulars, and a receipt must be attached to the return of election expenses.

Claims must be received within Fourteen Days after Election. As soon as possible after the election, the election agent should collect all outstanding accounts. If there is sufficient money in hand to allow of advertisements for claims, without exceeding the maximum, it may be desirable to give notice in this way to creditors.

All claims must be received by the election agent, or the sub-agent within whose district the claim was incurred, within fourteen days after the day on which the candidates returned are declared elected, otherwise the claims will be barred. If the claims are sent to any other person than those named, the sending in will be bad. They should be sent to the address of the election agent or sub-agent stated in the public notice given by the returning officer.

The provisions as to claims apply also to the election agent's remuneration ; to the candidate's statement of personal expenses paid by himself and the particulars of expenditure, if any, above the limit of £100; and to the statements of petty expenses paid by any persons under written authority from the election agent. These latter must be vouched for by a receipted bill giving particulars of the expenditure.

The returning officer is allowed twenty-one days after the day on which the candidates returned are declared elected in which to make his claim. He must render a detailed account showing the amounts of his charges, anc his claim must be transmitted to the election agent within the time specified.

The election agent must pay all claims which are not disputed by him within twenty-eight days after the day on which the candidates returned are declared elected. *Payment of Claims.*

Disputed claims fall under two heads :— *Disputed Claims.*

> (1) Where the liability is admitted, but the amount is disputed, and
>
> (2) Where liability is altogether disputed.

In each case the election agent must state, in his return of election expenses, particulars of such disputed claims, and give the names of the persons claiming. He must await the action of claimant in respect of any disputed claim.

Return and Declaration as to Expenses. The election agent must, within thirty-five days after the candidates returned are declared elected, transmit to the returning officer a return and declaration of the election expenses in the form prescribed by Schedule II., Part I., of the Corrupt Practices Act.

The declaration must be made before a Justice of the Peace.

DECLARATION AS TO EXPENSES BY ELECTION-AGENT.

Parliamentary Election for the ... of ... I ... being Election Agent to ... candidate at the election for the county [or borough] of ... on the ... day of ... do hereby solemnly and sincerely declare that I have examined the return of election expenses about to be transmitted by me to the Returning Officer at the said election, and now shown to me and marked ... and to the best of my knowledge and belief that return is correct;

And I hereby further solemnly and sincerely declare that, except as appears from that return, I have not and to the best of my knowledge and belief no other person, nor any club, society, or association has on behalf of the said Candidate made any payment, or given, promised, or offered any reward, office, employment, or valuable consideration, or incurred any liability on account of or in respect of the conduct or management of the said Election;

And I further solemnly and sincerely declare that I have received from the said Candidate ... pounds and no more [or nothing] for the purpose of the said Election, and that, except as specified in the said return sent by me, no money, security, or equivalent for money has been paid, advanced, given, or deposited by anyone to me or in my hands, or, to the best of my knowledge and belief, to or in the hands of any other person for the purpose of defraying any expenses incurred on behalf of the said Candidate on account of, or in respect of, the conduct or management of the said election.

Signature of Declarant ... Signed and declared by the above-named declarant on the ... day of ... before me.... (Signed) ... Justice of the Peace for ...

In computing the time allowed for sending in claims in respect of the election by persons other than the returning officer; for the payment of such claims; and also for transmitting the return and declaration respecting election expenses, it would appear that Sundays, Christmas Day, Good Friday, etc., must not be excluded. For example, if the declaration of the result of the election were made on Saturday, the 1st of the month, the last day for sending in claims to the election agent would be the 15th.

On the other hand, assuming the return to be made *i.e.* to have reached the Clerk of the Crown on Monday, the 3rd, the last day on which the returning officer may transmit his account to the election agent would be the 27th (Sundays, etc., being excluded in computing time in all matters in which the returning officer is concerned).

As the candidate is required to examine the accounts relating to the election before making his declaration in respect thereof, it would be well for the election agent to arrange, if possible, that the candidate's declaration should be sent in at the same time as he transmits the return and his own declaration.

ELECTION COMMITTEES.

THE formation of special election committees is attended by some risk, and is not free from other disadvantages arising out of the circumstance that every member of an election committee may be held to be an agent of the candidate.

On the other hand, it is certain that the aid of a willing and deeply interested committee is of the greatest value; and the influence of such a committee, if it be fully representative of all classes, will undoubtedly have a powerful effect upon the electorate.

The election agent should, therefore, at an early stage of the proceedings, consider whether the formation of such a committee is desirable, and, if desirable, possible.

In connection with the first of these considerations, the main point to be determined is whether the committee, if formed, is likely to render *active* assistance. A committee which exists only on paper is seldom of much use; at all events, the dangers in connection with such a committee are greater than the advantages.

The desirability of a committee having been determined upon, the election agent should at once test the possibility of forming it by inviting all the leading men of his party in the division to a preliminary meeting. It is not desirable that the election committee should be a very large body; but it is essential that it should be thoroughly representative of every shade of opinion. Probably it will be best in most cases to summon to the first meeting the officers of the district committees, *i.e.,* the chairmen and secretaries. At this meeting the election committee may be formally constituted, and its functions defined. The committee should have power to add to its number.

The election agent should submit to the meeting a brief outline of such schemes as he may have formulated, and should invite the co-operation of those present. He may also invite suggestions as to other matters, and a properly constituted committee can render invaluable assistance in connection with the organization of the campaign. The election agent should, however, make it clear to the committee at the outset that the acceptance of any suggestions made must depend not only upon their fitness, but upon their practicability in view of the general arrangements, and especially in regard to the expense involved.

It is a good plan to appoint the chairman and secretary of the election committee, an executive to consult with the election agent upon all matters of urgency.

Frequent meetings of the whole committee are very undesirable, as great waste of time is occasioned thereby.

Limitation of functions It has been pointed out that an election committee may render very important services ; but it appears necessary to add that the committee should be impressed with the fact that it has no right under the existing law to assume any administrative function. It should confine itself strictly to the organization of the district committees, and to deliberation and recommendation.. The election agent alone is responsible for administration and for the organization of his staff,. and on no account should the election committee attempt to interfere.

If in the opinion of the committee the election agent is negligent or incompetent, it may, of course, make any representation it thinks fit to the candidate, and, if he agrees with the committee, he may cancel the appointment of his agent.

Above all, the election committee must avoid incurring expenditure of any kind. The election agent is bound to keep strict control of financial matters, and it is illegal for a committee, or any member of it, to incur any expenditure on account of the election.

Organization of Local Committees. The first and most important duty of an election committee is to organize committees for the polling districts, or where committees exist in some districts and not in others to strengthen the weak places. The polling district committees will act under the direction of the sub-agent, and will conduct the canvass on behalf of their candidate. They should meet every night to report results and to decide upon methods of reaching doubtful voters.

The election committee may also form sub-committees to assist the election agent in arranging public meetings, and another sub-committee to assist in the preparation of leaflets, etc., etc., while yet another might usefully devote itself to securing promises of vehicles for use on the polling day.

Sub-committees.

Occasionally it may be found desirable to appoint a detective committee to collect evidence with reference to corrupt or illegal practices suspected or discovered. This committee should be small, and one member of it at least should be a lawyer who has a good knowledge of the locality and the people.

COMMITTEE-ROOMS.

THE number of committee-rooms that may be hired for payment in a county is limited as follows :—

> One central committee-room ;
>
> One committee-room for each polling district, and if the number of electors in a polling district exceeds 500, one additional committee-room for every *complete* 500 electors over and above the first 500.

There is no limit to the number of committee-rooms that may be used if they are gratuitously placed at the disposal of the candidate. The prohibited premises may not, however, be used under any circumstances.

The minimum number of committee-rooms required in a county election will be :—

> (1.) A central committee-room, which will be the election agent's address for the time being ;
>
> (2.) A committee-room for each sub-agent, which shall be the central office for

each group of polling districts, and must therefore afford sufficient accommodation for transacting all necessary business, holding meetings of the district committees, etc.; and

(3.) A committee-room in each polling district not already provided for under No. 2. These latter committee-rooms need not necessarily be open all day, but it is of the greatest importance that they should be open *for a stated time every evening in the week,* and that a responsible person should be in charge to answer inquiries and give information to all comers.

It is quite impossible to indicate with any approach to accuracy what should be paid for committee-rooms, but a word of caution may with advantage be given against paying the extortionate prices sometimes demanded during elections. It is undoubtedly desirable to obtain committee-rooms in a central and easily accessible position, but there is nearly always a second-best situation which may be made to serve the purposes of the agent almost equally well, and it is seldom that the whereabouts of the committee-room cannot by the exercise of a little ingenuity be made sufficiently clear.

Cost of Committee-rooms.

In selecting a central committee-room it is, however, of first importance that it should be in the town most easily accessible from all parts of

Situation of Central Committee-room.

the division, and the premises should be sufficiently commodious to afford facilities for the holding of committee meetings, and, if possible, to accommodate, in addition to the election agent's own staff, one of the sub-agents with his assistants.

Rooms required at Central Office. The election agent will require the following rooms :—

A large room for the use of canvassers and for committee meetings ;

A room for the out-voters' and removals' clerk and his assistants ;

A general clerk's room ; and on the ground floor—

An inquiry office and literature store-room.

Committee-rooms are prohibited on the following premises :—

Prohibited Premises. Premises licensed for the sale, wholesale or retail, of intoxicating liquors ; or on which intoxicating liquors *or refreshments of any kind, whether food or drink,* are supplied for consumption on the premises.

[An exception is made in favour of permanent political clubs, but it is best, as a rule, to avoid establishing committee-rooms in a club. The reasons are now pretty generally understood, and it is unnecessary to repeat them here.]

The premises which are prohibited, therefore, may be taken to include :—

Public-houses and hotels ;

Grocers' and other shops having licenses ;

The premises of brewers, wine and spirit merchants ;

Coffee and tea houses ; and certain
Confectioners' shops where refreshments
are supplied for consumption on the
premises.

Any part of such premises may, however, be
used for a committee-room if such part is
ordinarily let for chambers, offices, etc., *and
provided it has a separate entrance and no
direct communication with any part where
liquor is sold or refreshments supplied.*

It is, however, very unusual for such conditions to exist, and it is doubtful whether the
temporary closing and sealing of any passage
or other means of communication generally
existing would meet the requirements of the
Act.

An agent will, therefore, be well advised if he
avoid all risks in this matter.

Public elementary schools are also in the
list of places prohibited.

SUB-AGENTS.

GREAT care should be exercised in the selection of sub-agents. It should be remembered that they are deputy election agents, and that any indiscretion or illegal act committed by them will have the same effect as if committed by the election agent himself.

Casual attention to duties an evil.

It has been the custom in the past to appoint as sub-agents persons who have thought it sufficient to attend to the work of the election during the brief intervals when their own business or profession did not press for their attention. It cannot be too strongly urged that in the future this practice should be abandoned, except in very special cases; and that every man who receives an appointment as sub-agent should enter into an agreement to devote his whole time and thoughts to the duties of his office during a period specified by the election agent.

Importance of Sub-agent's work.

The sub-agent's functions are only second in importance to those of the election agent himself. He is responsible for the proper working of the districts assigned to him. Where there are good local committees to assist him his work will, of course, be comparatively light ; but even under the most favourable circumstances he has opportunity for the display of energy and ability, which may have an important effect upon the result.

In most county divisions the number of polling districts has been considerably increased of late. These additions, while a great convenience to voters, necessitate a slight alteration in the organization of an election staff—an alteration which has, however, been adopted for some time past by the most experienced agents in county elections. Instead of a sub-agent having charge of one polling district only, two or three districts are grouped together, and a man of experience put in charge of the group. Eight to ten sub-agents can efficiently work a division containing twenty to thirty polling districts.

Grouping of Polling Districts.

Assuming, therefore, that a sub-agent is appointed to work three polling districts, his first business will be to secure, if that has not already been done, a committee - room conveniently situated as a centre from which the work of the three districts can be directed, and also committee - rooms in each of the other polling districts.

Matters requiring immediate attention.

He will then summon committee meetings for the earliest possible date in each of his districts.

If the canvass books and street lists have

not been made out, he must at once put this
work in hand, and will proceed according to the
instructions previously given in this manual.

He should also find out what places are available for public meetings, and arrange terms
with the proprietors. He cannot, of course, fix
definitely the dates for meetings without instructions from the election agent ; but he should
ascertain not only when the buildings are free,
but the days on which it is desirable to hold
meetings.

The number of meetings to be held will
depend upon the speakers available, and, to
some extent, upon the conditions under which
the election is being held. The meetings of the
local committees will, of course, afford him an
opportunity for obtaining much information on
this and other points.

Having obtained full particulars, he should at
once report them to the election agent.

Copies of Register required. Prior to the meeting of the committees the
sub-agent should be provided with one complete
register of electors in the division, and also with
the portion of the register applying to each of
the districts under his control.

The complete register he should keep at his
own committee-room for reference and for
marking up for the use of the personation
agent. The district lists he will, of course, hand
over to the secretary of the local committee or
other person in charge of the committee-room.

The sub-agent should invariably attend the first meeting of the local committees, and he should be prepared to allot to each member of the committee as much work as it will be in his power to do during the next two or three days. What this work will be will, of course, depend upon the state of preparedness for an election existing in the constituency. But assuming that the canvass books are ready, as they ought to be, they should be distributed and the canvass begun forthwith.

In many districts an objection to canvassing prevails amongst the members of the committee, but it is quite certain that this objection is not shared by the majority of the voters, excepting, perhaps, in some very few districts where the system has become obnoxious through the tyranny, or persecution, resorted to in connection with it by some misguided partisans. In these exceptional cases, however, it may be taken for granted that the bulk of the inhabitants will take revenge on those who have sought to interfere with their freedom by voting for the opposite party. In ordinary cases it cannot be too strongly impressed on the local committee that the prospects of their candidate will be improved or impaired, according to the efficiency, or otherwise, of the canvass. It must always be borne in mind that nine out of every ten Englishmen will keep a promise once definitely made. This is

Canvassing.

not a random statement, but is founded upon the
experience afforded by many elections. It follows
from this that a further advantage may be gained
by promptness in beginning and energy in
prosecuting the canvass. The committee-men
should be asked to use every effort to see voters
personally—never to be satisfied, in fact, until
they have done so—and at least twice a week
the committee should meet for the purpose of
reporting progress in the canvass. It is not
necessary, or even desirable, that all the members
of the committee should be present while the
canvass report is being made. It is much better
that the proceedings should commence, say, at
eight o'clock, with such members as happen to
be present, and be conducted in an informal
manner. In this way there is the minimum of
interference with the progress of the canvass.
When a full meeting is held doubtful names can
be called over and allotted to those members of
the committee who are considered best qualified
to deal with them.

Special attention should be directed by the
sub-agent to these doubtful voters, and also to
removed voters. A plan of dealing with the
latter is discussed later on.

All particulars of the canvass should be entered
in the district canvass registers, or street lists, as
they are sometimes called, and the sub-agent
ought to be in a position to send in daily to the

election agent a summary of the results showing some progress. The following is a useful form for this purpose :—

CANVASS RETURN FOR . . . POLLING DISTRICT.

For . . . day . . . —th, 189 . This return to be sent regularly to Mr. . . . Central Committee Rooms.

Polling District No.	For.	Against.	Favourable	Doubtful.	Neutral.	Dead.	Removed.	No. Accounted for.	No on Register.	No. to Account for.

Before leaving the subject of canvassing it may be well to allude to a method by which the difficulty, often met with in country districts, of canvassing the scattered voters, may be overcome.

Canvassing Voters in outlying districts.

A waggonette or other conveyance should be obtained to take out small parties who are willing to undertake the canvass. The route should be carefully chosen by someone familiar with the district, and a member of the party dropped from time to time at a convenient spot near a group of houses. In this way a large area can be covered in two or three hours and much valuable work done. A rendezvous should be appointed where all can meet at a given hour and be driven back to the committee-room.

On no account should the outlying voters be neglected. If nothing else can be done, small packets of leaflets or other literature should be posted to them from time to time ; but it is undoubtedly better that they should, if possible, be personally visited. The visiting parties should always take with them a supply of leaflets, and it is a good plan to arrange these beforehand into little packets of half-a-dozen or so on different subjects.

Committee-rooms to be open every day. Of course the district committee-rooms should be open every day, for the whole day, if possible, but, at the very least, for some hours in the evening, and the chairman or some person of authority and experience should be in charge to give advice and information to all needing them.

Advertising Meetings. Upon the sub-agent will rest the responsibility for the meetings within his districts. He must take care that all arrangements are properly made, and that the meetings are well advertised. Usually at a general election there is ample time to get out bills and distribute them, and it is not necessary to detail the arrangements necessary in a bye-election when the pressure is much greater and all movements must be accelerated.

As a rule it is absolutely useless, and, therefore, a waste of money, to advertise meetings in the newspapers in counties. Large posters also should be very sparingly used for this purpose; they are expensive, and the places where they may be posted up are very few in number. In fact, as a rule, they are entirely unnecessary. The best way of proclaiming meetings in most

places is by the distribution from house to house
of small handbills stating —

    (*a*) The town or village where the meeting
        is to be held ;

    (*b*) The place of assembly ;

    (*c*) The date of the meeting [giving both
        day of week and day of month] ;

    (*d*) The time of beginning ;

    (*e*) The names of the chairman and principal
        speakers ; and

    (*f*) A bold announcement of the name of the
        candidate in whose support the meet-
        ing is to be held.

These matters are mentioned because handbills and posters are so frequently spoiled and
rendered useless when drawn up by inexperienced
persons owing to the omission of one or other
point of importance.

The sub-agent should examine a proof of every
bill issued, and take particular notice that each
one bears the imprint of the printer and publisher.

The handbills should be distributed three or
four days, but not more than a week, beforehand,
unless very special circumstances demand longer
notice.

If necessary the services of the crier may be
requisitioned to supplement the other plan of
advertisement, and on an emergency this func-
tionary may be entrusted with the whole burden
of spreading the news.

Arrangements at place of meeting. The arrangements in connection with the room in which the meeting is to be held should be carefully attended to. Everything, from the doorkeeper to the waterbottle, should be in position some time before the hour announced for the chairman to take his place; nothing should be left to chance, and no one should be in a state of uncertainty. It is on small matters that the success or failure of meetings in villages and the lesser towns mainly depends.

Subagents and attendance at meetings. While the sub-agent should master every detail in connection with meetings, and should personally see that everything is in order, it is very undesirable that he should, except in an emergency, devote any great portion of his time to attending them. There is so much detail work to attend to that he can seldom spare the time; and as the same may be said of most members of the local committees, it is very necessary that the sub-agent should, by example as well as precept, do all in his power to secure the strict attention of all to the committee-room and canvassing work. There will, of course, be exceptions to this rule; but in the main it may be taken as desirable to adhere to it with some strictness.

Poll Cards. Usually in counties the candidate's poll cards are sent to the sub-agents to be filled up and distributed. In such cases if the sub-agent has not received his share of the cards within 24 hours of the time when he knows the necessary information as to the polling stations fixed by the returning officer must have reached the election agent, he should at once make inquiry about the cards. He will have to arrange for members of the committee or other voluntary assistants to fill up the cards, and sometimes to address envelopes. In any case it will be necessary to carefully correct addresses according to information obtained during the canvass. If this is not done, or is done carelessly, it is obvious that many voters will never receive their poll cards, much trouble and some waste of votes thereby arising. All this requires time, and it is important, therefore, that the sub-agent should be able to get the work in hand early.

Sometimes the poll cards are handed over to the canvassers for distribution, and where there are strong committees, the members of which can be relied upon to do the work thoroughly and without delay, no better plan can be adopted. It has the advantage of enabling the canvassers to have a last word with the electors on the eve of the poll, besides reducing the postage account. If, however, the committees are weak and could not cover the ground thoroughly, it is far better to send the cards, or the bulk of them, by post. It is safe to say that in the latter case the cards should be posted in counties never less than two days before the opening of the poll, and in some exceptional instances even three days should be allowed. When they are delivered by the canvassers the same rule as to time may generally be applied with advantage.

The election agent will have directed what enclosures shall go with the poll card, and should have sent a full supply in good time.

Clerks, Messengers, and Personation Agents. Probably the sub-agent will be required to engage his own clerks and messengers, and to find personation agents for the day of poll. In this case he must take care that the latter make the statutory declaration before the opening of the poll, and that they receive in due time their appointments, marked lists, and instructions, and also that notice of their appointment is duly forwarded to the returning officer or to the election agent for him to send on. If the sub-agent is required to attend the counting he must also remember that he has to make the declaration before a Justice of the Peace.

Personation Agent's Lists. Prior to the polling day the sub-agent must prepare marked lists for his personation agent's use. These lists should be marked up as far as possible under his own supervision, and should contain information carefully verified as to all persons reported " dead," " gone abroad," " too ill to vote," " cannot be traced." Duplicate entries should also be carefully marked.

Other preparations for Day of Poll. He should also prepare lists of voluntary assistants, and carriages promised, and should allot them to their various stations. Checkers should also be appointed to stand near the entrance to the polling stations and report from time to time,.

on slips provided for the purpose, the names of voters who have polled. The checkers, if paid, should be selected from the staff of clerks or messengers already engaged. Cards for canvassers' use should also be written up in readiness. These cards should contain the names and addresses of all those who have promised their support or who are believed to be favourable, and should be used instead of the canvass books.

If there are any voters who have not been seen their names should be put on separate cards. Each card should contain six or eight names.

In some places the plan is still followed of posting the register on large card-boards and marking the names of those who have promised support; but it is suggested that this plan not only involves a lot of unnecessary trouble, but is also undesirable in other ways. For instance, the sheet is a conspicuous object, and is almost of necessity open to the inspection of any person who enters the committee-room. In this way an opponent may obtain information which can be used to the prejudice of electors. All this trouble and risk may be obviated by the use of the district register or street list already mentioned, which should be placed in the hands of the clerk or other person in charge of the committee-room, and by him marked up as the reports are received from canvassers and checkers. The work. can be got through quite as expeditiously in this way as in any other, and there are none of the disadvantages attendant upon the wall-sheet method.

Carriages   Particular care should be taken in the organization of the vehicular service, not to waste the resources at the disposal of the agent.   A plan of working the vehicles is suggested under a separate heading.   This plan should be explained beforehand to the committees, and strictly adhered to on the polling day.

Close of the Poll.   At the close of the poll the sub-agent should obtain the books from the district committee-room, and the lists from his personation agents, and having cast up the results should forward the totals immediately by telegram or messenger to the election agent.

It is impossible to go into further detail with regard to a sub-agent's duties without unduly extending this chapter.   The main points have been dealt with, and for the rest a sub-agent should acquaint himself with the provisions of the Corrupt Practices Act affecting those matters with which he is concerned, and should also study the instructions which in a previous chapter it is suggested should be issued by the election agent.

If a sub-agent is in doubt at any time upon any subject, he should consult the election agent.

Special points to be remembered.   The things he should specially bear in mind are —

    (1.) That neither he himself nor any clerk, messenger, or personation agent

being an elector and receiving payment for his services, may vote in the
election.

(2.) That any act or default of a sub-agent
within his district will be deemed to
be the act or default of the election
agent and will entail the same consequences.

(3.) That he is bound, not only to avoid all
illegal and corrupt practices himself,
but to take all means in his power to
prevent others from committing them.
He should, therefore, cause to be
displayed in every committee-room
under his control a list of corrupt
and illegal practices with the penalties
attending them, and, whenever it
appears necessary, take other steps
to warn those who appear to need it.

(4.) That all the information he collects with
reference to the canvass should be
kept secret ; and he should be particularly careful not to disclose to
anyone the names of persons who
have promised to vote for the candidate in whose interest he is acting.
He would also do well to counsel
discretion in this respect by his canvassers.

(5.) That he must on no account incur expense beyond the amount authorized
by the election agent in writing ; and

that no member of the committee or other person, except a clerk acting under his instructions, may make any payment whatever.

(6.) That all books, lists, and other papers relating to the election must be collected immediately the election is over and forwarded by him to the election agent.

(7.) That all accounts outstanding within his district must be collected within 14 days after the candidate returned is declared elected. It is best that the sub-agent should pay all these accounts himself, but if from any cause this cannot be done, they should be forwarded immediately to the election agent. The sub-agent's claim for remuneration must be sent in within the 14 days allowed.

(8). That a detailed account and a receipt are necessary for all bills amounting to 40s. and upwards.

CLERKS AND MESSENGERS.

For the number who may be employed, see p. 28.

The functions of clerks and messengers are of a general character. They may be employed in any polling district where their services are required.

No elector employed in either capacity for payment may vote. This provision extends to employment within six months of the election; violation of it is a misdemeanour.

As regards messengers, it may be desirable to call attention to the great saving of time and labour that may be made by the employment of expert bicycle riders. Rapid communication may be effected in this way with distant parts of the county at a very small cost as compared with that incurred when a horse and trap are used.

PERSONATION AGENTS.

NOTHING is more difficult, as a rule, than to get efficient personation agents, and yet few persons engaged in an election occupy a more important position. The polling agent is the only person on the day of the poll who has the opportunity of watching, on behalf of a candidate, the proceedings within the polling station. It is his duty not only to see that personation is prevented ; but to see that the provisions of the Ballot Act are enforced by the presiding officer.

One personation agent, and no more, may be appointed to a polling station on behalf of each candidate ; and he must make a declaration of secrecy before entering the booth.

He should have a knowledge of the Ballot Act and should carefully study the instructions handed to him by or on behalf of the election agent. If possible a man in whom the voters have confidence should be selected, and it is of importance that he should himself possess an intimate knowledge of the electors individually. While it is his duty to prevent personation and fraud, it is no less incumbent upon him to secure the observance of the provisions of the Ballot Act intended for the protection of the voters against intimidation and interference. It is essential, therefore, that he should be a man of firmness and decision If he has occasion to call the attention of the presiding officer to illegalities or irregularities of any kind, or to remonstrate with him, and if his representations are without effect, he should at once communicate with the returning officer requesting his intervention. If the returning officer is not within his reach he should communicate with the election agent or the candidate on whose behalf he is acting.

Forms of declaration and notice to returning officers will be found on page 32.

COUNTING AGENTS.

THESE must be selected from amongst the sub-agents or other officials employed, and their number may, if desired, be augmented by volunteers nominated by the candidate. Their duties vary in detail according to the system of counting adopted by the returning officer; but their function is to watch the ballot papers on behalf of the candidate in whose interest they are acting.

They must make the declaration of secrecy, and their appointment must be made and notified to the returning officer one clear day before the poll.

Should not leave table to which assigned.
They should be instructed by the election agent to take their places at particular tables, and on no account to move from their places until the counting is finished. In some cases the returning officer insists upon this course being followed; but in any case the rule should be strictly observed.

Counting agents should bear in mind the following points, and should see that the officials in no way violate the rules laid down by the Ballot Act in relation to them :—

(1.) Before proceeding with the counting of the votes the returning officer must, *in the presence of the agents of the candidate,* open each ballot box and count and record the number of voting papers contained in it. All the papers should be accounted for.

(2.) The papers should be counted *face upwards.* This is a provision expressly made by Rule 34 of the Ballot Act, and is designed to prevent any person from seeing the number on the back of the ballot paper. It is usual for returning officers to provide an official stamp for the marking of the ballot papers, which *perforates* the paper, and this to a great extent obviates the necessity for examining the back. Where a perforating stamp is not used of course all duly appointed persons are entitled to see that the official mark is on the back of each paper ; but no one is permitted under any circumstances to take note of the number. The official presiding at the table should take such precau-

tions as may seem necessary to prevent this.

(3.) When the papers have been thus verified
the contents of all the ballot boxes
must be mixed together, and the
counting of the votes will then be
proceeded with.

(4). Ballot papers are void and are not to be
counted :—

(a) Which have not on the back
the official mark.

(b) On which votes are recorded
for more candidates than the
voter is entitled to vote for.

(c) On which any mark or writing
is made by which it would
be possible for the voter to
be identified.

Disputed Votes. When a counting agent detects any infringement of these rules, or sees a paper so marked
that it is doubtful for which candidate the elector
intended to vote, he must at once challenge
the paper, which will then be put aside for the
consideration of the returning officer.

A simple method of Counting. Very often the candidate's counting agent has
no part in the actual recording of the number
of votes ; but in a very admirable system adopted
by some returning officers he is furnished
with a book containing parallel slips with the
name of each candidate at the top. These slips
have each 100 lines or spaces, and, as the official

presiding at the table opens the ballot paper and calls out the name of the candidate voted for, each person at the table makes a mark in one of the spaces until the bottom of the slip is reached, when " check " is called and the slip (which is perforated) is turned over. When all the votes have been counted it is easy to cast up the totals at each table ; and as the count has been checked during its progress it is almost impossible for any error to have occurred.

When other methods are adopted the ballot papers are usually put together in fifties and passed up to the returning officer's table.

Counting agents should bear in mind that they are bound to aid in maintaining the secrecy of the ballot, and they must not, therefore, attempt to ascertain how any voter has voted, nor must they, if they can prevent it, allow any other person to do so.

There is no provision for the payment of counting agents, but if they are selected from the paid staff they must not vote.

NOMINATION.

Notice of
Election.
Nomina-
tion
Papers to
be pro-
vided by
Return-
ing
Officer. THE notice of election must be given by the returning officer in a county within two days after the day on which he receives the writ; and during two hours, fixed by the returning officer, between 10 a.m. and 2 p.m. on each day intervening between the notice of election and the day fixed for the nomination, forms of nomination must be given by the returning officer, free of charge, to any registered elector applying for the same. The place at which the forms are obtainable is notified by the returning officer, and should be a place convenient for the electors.

The election agent should see that a sufficient number of forms is obtained.

Number
of nomin-
ations
that may
be made. There is no limit to the number of nominations that may be handed in, and it is very desirable that more than one paper should be filled up. But, on the other hand, it is often the case

that an excessive number of nominations is made.

A good rule to make in connection with this matter is that nominations should be handed in on behalf of such important classes of electors as may exist within the division. Where this rule is observed five or six forms will usually be found ample. There is no object in sending in more, and any excess only causes needless trouble and waste of time.

The candidate must be described in such a manner as, in the opinion of the returning officer, is sufficient to identify him. His surname must come first, and his other names must be given in full. A candidate being an Irish peer, or bearing a courtesy title, may be described by his title as if it were his surname. In the case of a candidate bearing a compound surname, it would appear to be correct to insert his surname in the way he ordinarily writes it, *i.e.*, the first name of the compound first. The candidate's description shall include his names, his abode, and his rank, profession, or calling. *Candidate's description.*

The following suggestions are offered as to the method of filling up nomination papers in certain cases :— *Suggestions for filling up papers.*

Parliamentary Election for the . . . Division of the County of . . . 189 .

We, the undersigned . . . of . . . in the County of . . . and . . . of . . . in the County of . . . being registered electors of the said County, do hereby nominate the following person as a proper person to serve as Member for the said Division of the County of . . . in Parliament.

G

Surname.	Other Names.	Abode.	Rank, Profession, or Occupation.
BROWN	John...	52, George St., Bristol	Merchant
JONES	*or* William David	High Elms, Wilts	Esquire
MERTON	*or* Hon. George Travis, commonly called Viscount	Swanworth, Berks	Viscount
SMITH	*or* Henry Sydney	72, High St., Bath	Attorney

(Signed)   A. B.
                                                C. D.

We, the undersigned, being registered electors of the County of . . .
do hereby assent to the nomination of the above-mentioned . . . as
a proper person to serve as Member for the said . . . Division of the
County of . . . in Parliament. (Signed) EDWARD FRANKS, of
Hollybrook, Rainham—and seven other persons, making eight assentors
in all.

Signatures of Nominators and Assentors.

The nominators and assentors should sign their
names and give their addresses as they appear
in the register of electors, or if the address on
the register is not at the time correct, the present
address should be stated and the words "late
of," etc., added, and the election agent should
carefully check all the papers with the register
before allowing them to be handed in to the
returning officer. It will be found a convenience
to the officials and will save time if he writes
with a pencil the register number of each nomi-
nator and assentor against his name.

The election agent must bear in mind that the electors signing the nomination paper should not only be on the register, but should be clearly qualified to be thereon ; otherwise the nomination may be bad.

The nomination is not bad if one of the persons signing has not written his name in full. The ordinary signature is sufficient ; but it is desirable that the names should be written in full and as given in the register.

The nomination paper must be filled up before any signature is attached, and the nominators must sign first and the eight assentors afterwards.

The same elector may not sign more nomination papers than there are vacancies to be filled.

The candidate, his proposer and seconder, and one other person to be named by the candidate, are entitled to attend the nomination. *Who are entitled to attend Nominations.*

Nomination papers must be handed to the returning officer by the candidate himself, or by his proposer or seconder, *and not by an agent.*

Objections to nomination papers may be made before the expiration of the time appointed for the election, or within one hour afterwards ; but no objection to a nomination paper on the ground of the description of the candidate therein being insufficient or not being in compliance with Rule 6 of the Ballot Act, shall be allowed or deemed valid unless such objection is made by the returning officer, or by some other *Objections to Nomination Papers.*

person, *at or immediately after* the time of the delivery of the nomination paper.

The following are examples of the grounds on which objection may be made to a nomination paper:—

(1.) Insufficient or inaccurate description of the candidate.

> *Objections on this ground must be made immediately after the delivery of the nomination paper to the returning officer.*

(2.) That the candidate is not a natural born subject.

(3.) That he is not of full age.

(4.) That he is ineligible for Parliament, being subject to one of the disqualifications mentioned in the chapter on candidates.

(5.) That one or more of the nominators or assentors is not on, or entitled to be on the register of electors.

Who may object. The objection may be made either by the returning officer or one of the persons entitled to be present at the nomination. It is not clear whether any other person has a right to object before the expiration of the time fixed for the election; but it would appear that during the one hour after that time during which the returning officer must sit to hear objections any elector may object on any ground except the first-named.

It is well to reserve objections on any ground except No. 1 until after the expiration of the time for handing in nominations, as in the event of the objection being then sustained the objecting candidate might claim the seat.

It has been held in some municipal cases that the returning officer has no power to deal with objections that attack the qualification of the candidate (see Pritchard v. Mayor of Bangor, 13 App. Cases, pp. 251, 257); but if there is good reason for raising objection on the ground of the ineligibility of the candidate, it would be desirable to object, even though the returning officer may decline to entertain it.

Care should be taken not to object on any ground without good reason. Frivolous objections not only waste time, but may entail even more serious consequences.

If the returning officer disallows an objection his decision is final, and if he allows it his decision is only subject to reversal on petition questioning the election or return.

The candidate or his election agent must be prepared to give security for the returning officer's charges, if required, in any legal tender or otherwise as may be decided by the returning officer. The election agent should, therefore, ascertain beforehand in what form the required security will be desired, i.e., whether in gold, notes, or cheque.

OUTVOTERS AND REMOVALS.

THE proper working of this department is one of the most important matters claiming the attention of the election agent. In many counties the outvoters form a very considerable proportion of the electorate, whilst in the case of an election on an old register the removals often number many hundreds.

It is obvious, therefore, that much may depend upon the attention given to these classes of voters, and more especially the removals.

The election agent will consequently appoint one of the most capable members of his staff to supervise this work; and he may be assisted by a small committee.

OUTVOTERS.

Canvassing outvoters. In order that these may be canvassed it is necessary to extract their names from the register. This should be done on sheets, a form of which is suggested below. Each sheet should contain the names of voters residing in the same Division, and the party agent responsible for the organization of the Division should be requested to

report upon every name. It is of course imperative that this canvass should be voluntary.

The following form may be used :—

Parliamentary Election for the . . . Division of the County of . . .
Mr. . . . Central Committee Rooms.

To Mr. . . . The persons whose names are given below reside in your
district but are entitled to vote in this Division. You will greatly help
us if you will canvass these Voters and report the result to me not later
than . . . (Signed) . . .

Name.	Address.	Situation of qualifying Property.	Politics.		Will Vote.	Will not Vote.	Remarks.
			C.	L.			

The reports having been received, and the
particulars extracted, the agent should as soon
as possible send either the ordinary poll-card or
a letter similar to the one drafted below, with
the form attached, to each voter reported as
having promised his support, and it may be well
to send also to those as to whom no report is
made.

Communicating with Out-voters who have promised support.

Parliamentary Election for the . . . Division of the County of . . .
Mr. . . . Central Committee Rooms.

Dear Sir,—On behalf of the Liberal Candidate, Mr. . . . I ven-
ture to appeal for your vote at the present Election. The Polling
Day is fixed for . . . day . . . and your Polling Station is at . . .
If it would add to your convenience, I will endeavour to send
a conveyance to meet you at your Station of arrival on receiving *early*
information of your intention and wish. Further than this I have no
power to go, as the Corrupt Practices Act of 1883 forbids, under serious
penalties, any payment by a Candidate or his Agents for railway fare
or the conveyance of Electors to or from the Poll. I enclose form, with
addressed and stamped envelope, for reply, and am, Dear Sir, yours
faithfully . . . Election Agent.

FORM OF REPLY.

To Mr. . . . Dear Sir, it is my intention to vote for Mr. . . . on
. I shall arrive at . . . Station at . . . *and shall be glad if you will
send a conveyance to meet me. Yours truly (Sd.) . . . Address . . .

*Strike out these words if a carriage is not required.

REMOVALS.

In a perfectly organized Division the work of following up removals will be always kept well in hand. Each member of a Polling District Committee will have been furnished with a little book containing twenty or thirty slips similar to the one here shown :—

No. 1.—REMOVALS TRACED PREVIOUS TO ELECTION.

. . . Polling District.   Name of outgoing tenant . . . removed from . . . to . . . Date of Removal . . . Politics . . . Name of incoming tenant . . . removed from . . . to . . . Date of Removal . . . Politics . . . Signed . . . Canvasser.

The particulars will have been reported at the periodical meetings of the committees, and entered up in books kept for the purpose at the central office.

In such a case whenever an election comes the task of dealing with removals will be comparatively simple, however large the number may be.

Assuming, however, that such preparations have not been made, it will be necessary to collect information with the utmost possible despatch.

Removals may be divided into two classes :—

(1.) Those who have removed from one polling district to another within the same County Division ; and

(2.) Those who have removed outside the Division altogether.

It will simplify the work if the first class is dealt with by the sub-agents themselves communicating one with another, but all voters coming in the second should be dealt with at the central committee-room.

The canvassers' reports will afford a large *Post-office returns.* amount of information with reference to removals, and sub-agents and clerks in charge of committee-rooms should make a daily return of all instances discovered. The returns through the Dead Letter Office when the candidate's address has been posted to the electors will also afford much valuable information.

It will, perhaps, be most convenient if the *Plan of working at Central Committee-room.* work to be done at the Central Committee-room is first described, and that to be performed by the sub-agents discussed later on. As the Post-office returns come in they should be carefully sorted over, and particulars forwarded to the sub-agents in whose districts the voter's qualification exists, with the following note and form :—

No. 2.—REMOVALS—POST-OFFICE RETURNS.

Parliamentary Election for the . . . Division of the County of . . . Central Committee Room . . . 189 . The Election Address sent to the undermentioned Electors has been returned by the Post-office authorities marked "Left." Kindly have a special canvass made with the object of ascertaining whether any error has been made by the Post-office Officials, and of finding out as far as may be possible where the removed Voters are now residing.

Reg. No.	Name.	Removed from.	To.

Where the voter's new address has been *Removals outside Parliamentary Division.* ascertained and it is found to be outside the Parliamentary Division the names should at once be forwarded to the party agents in the district to which the voters have removed.

The following form may be used, and will, of course, apply also to the voters reported from time to time by the sub-agents as having removed into other Parliamentary Divisions :—

No. 3.—REMOVALS.

Parliamentary Election for the . . . Division of the County of . . .
To . . .   Central Committee-room.

....

....

The undermentioned persons having a qualification in this Division are reported as having removed into your district. I should be greatly obliged if you would have them canvassed, and any information you are able to obtain as to the present address, politics, and intentions of the voter marked upon this form, which should be returned to me at the earliest possible date.

No. on Register	Name of Elector.	Address on Register.	Removed to.	Politics. L.	C.	Remarks. (a) Whether Elector intends to vote. (b) Whether he desires to be met at station. (c) Time of his arrival, etc., etc., etc.

Where the voter's new address is within the same Parliamentary Division particulars should be forwarded to the sub-agent *from whose district the voter has removed*, and he will institute the necessary inquiries on a similar form.

Traced Removals. The removals clerk will, of course, keep a record of all replies received to his inquiries, and also forward to the sub-agents from whose districts the voters have removed all information he is able to get concerning them. A traced removals form is shown below :—

Parliamentary Election for the . . . Division of the County of . . .
No. 4.—TRACED REMOVALS. POLLING DISTRICT . . .

Reg. No.	Name.	Politics.		Removed from.	Present Address.	Remarks.
		L.	C.			

He must also arrange with the party agents in the various Divisions where removed voters are residing, that on the polling day the said voters shall be canvassed in the same way as though they were still living within the constituency where they are entitled to vote. On the polling day he should keep up communications with the various agents until he learns that every voter is known to be on his way to the polling booth, or that from some unpreventable cause he is absolutely unable to record his vote.

As regards removals from one polling district to another within the same Parliamentary Division, with which it is suggested the sub-agents should deal direct between themselves, the following is a sketch of the plan that should be adopted:—

Removals within the Parliamentary Division.

In most cases of removal reported the canvassers will have been able to make some statement as to the place where the voter has gone to reside. It will then be the business of the sub-agent to see that the name of the voter is at once sent on to the sub-agent within whose district the voter now lives, with a request that he shall be canvassed and reported on (see Removals Form, No. 3). When no information as to the new ad-

dress is forthcoming at first the name should be
sent to every sub-agent within the Parliamentary
Division with a request that full inquiry shall be
made as to whether such a person has come to
reside in his district. At the same time, of
course, no effort should be spared to find out
some neighbour who can give information as to
where the removed voter has gone.

Where a canvass thus organized is thoroughly
carried out, almost every removal can be traced ;
any voter not found should be specially marked
on the personation agent's list, and if he presents
himself to vote the presiding officer should be
asked to put the usual questions to him.

Polling
Removals.
In the case of removals reported upon as
pledged to vote in favour of the candidate in
whose interest he has been canvassed, pains
should be taken to ascertain whether it is
necessary to convey him to the poll ; and if so
the sub-agent into whose district he has removed
should, generally speaking, undertake the responsibility of sending a vehicle to take him to the
polling place and bring him back again. This
is obviously the best plan, as it saves one journey
out and back again, as compared with an arrangement by which the voter is sent for by the agent
for the district where he is to poll and then driven
back to his home.

Of course it will be borne in mind that no
railway, 'bus, or tram fares may be paid, and
that no horse or vehicle ordinarily let for hire
may be employed to convey voters to the poll.

CONVEYANCES.

THE Corrupt Practices Act of 1883 makes it illegal

> (a) To make any payment or contract for Illegal Expenditure. payment before, during, or after an election on account of the conveyance of voters to or from the poll.

The only exception is with regard to the very rare cases in which at a county election resident electors are unable to reach their polling place without crossing the sea. In these cases the candidate may provide the means for conveying them *by sea* to record their votes; but no vehicle may be hired for the purpose of completing the journey on land, nor, to all appearance, may boats be hired to convey them back again.

Any payment made under this exception is in addition to the amount allowed by the maximum scale.

> (b.) To " let, lend, or employ," or to "hire borrow, or use," for conveying electors to the poll, any *carriage, horse.*

or other animal ordinarily kept or used for the purpose of letting out for hire.—C. P. A., Sec. 14.

It is therefore illegal to *use* for the conveyance of voters to the poll any horse or carriage ordinarily let out for hire by any person, even if such horse or carriage is offered gratuitously by the owner.

Any elector, or several electors, may hire for his or their own use, and at his sole or their joint cost, any vehicle in which to go to the poll; but they may not take with them any elector who does not bear his due share of the expense.

It is also illegal to pay the railway, omnibus, or tramway fares of any elector going to the poll.

Vehicles mav be lent. There is nothing, however, to prevent any person owning a vehicle or animal which is *not* ordinarily let out for hire, lending such vehicle or animal for use on the polling day, provided, of course, that no payment or promise of payment is made. Neither does the prohibition of the other vehicles mentioned affect their use previously to the day of the poll for the purposes of the election.

Use of Vehicles prior to Day of Poll. As regards the use of vehicles prior to the day of election it is impossible to say much by way of guidance, owing to the widely differing circumstances under which elections are fought. In some counties the railway facilities are good, while in others they scarcely exist; in some instances in the North of England there is a network of tramways and a frequent service of other public conveyances, rendering the employment of special carriages almost unnecessary. Again, at bye-elections there is a much greater demand for carriages than at a general election, rendering it necessary in the former case to adopt a special system of dealing with the vehicular service. Agents will, however, do well to bear in mind that carriage hire is expensive, and should, therefore, be closely watched. It should be intimated to all jobmasters and others hiring out carriages and horses that no claim made by them will be recognized or paid unless it can be vouched for by an order bearing the signature of the election agent or a sub-agent.

As regards the procuring, allotting, and management of vehicles lent by friends of the candidate for use on the polling day it will be desirable to make the arrangements with some care. There is often a painful wear and tear of horse-flesh and waste of energy in connection with the vehicular service, most of which might be obviated by the observance of a few simple rules.

Management of Carriages on Day of Poll.

In the first place, the carriages sub-committee, if there be one, or the clerk in charge of the carriage department, should ascertain beforehand how many vehicles are likely to be placed at their disposal in each polling district. If there be an excess in any district or districts and a deficiency in others the needful steps should be taken to adjust the difference, so that every district will be fairly supplied.

At each committee-room there should be one person whose sole duty it will be to regulate the service from that committee-room, and no one should be allowed to take away a carriage without instructions are given by that person.

The clerk in charge of the committee-room should extract from his district register particulars as to those electors who have expressed a desire for a carriage to be sent for them. These particulars should be put on slips and arranged on an ordinary bill file in time order. Thus, those who are to be fetched at eight o'clock would come first, half-past eight following in order, and so on. The slips should be passed out at the proper time to the vehicle superintendent, who should then despatch a carriage for the voter, the driver or a canvasser accompanying him being requested to report at the committee-room when the elector has polled. Should the voter not keep his appointment the slip should be passed back into the committee-room and placed on another file, to be dealt with at a fitting opportunity later in the day.

Main points to be observed. A system of this kind is, of course, subject to modifications in practice, but the main points to be insisted upon are —

1. That the vehicles shall be under the control of the sub-agent or his deputy *in* the committee-room, and of the carriage superintendent *outside* the committee-room ;

2. That voters known to require fetching at stated times shall receive first attention ; and

3. That irresponsible persons shall not be allowed to take vehicles on wild-goose chases after voters who do not desire a conveyance, or who, for aught the impetuous canvasser knows, may have polled hours previously.

The carriage superintendent should be carefully instructed as to polling removals from other districts upon the plan described in a previous chapter. The natural tendency of canvassers is to go in search of voters whom they know have removed from their own district into some other, but it has been shown how great a waste of time and resources is involved in such a course. *Polling removals.*

There is usually a slack time on every election day, and advantage should be taken of this to rest the horses in view of the heavy demands made on their strength during the latter part of the day.

PUBLIC MEETINGS.

Manage-
ment of
Meetings. IT has already been suggested that a thoroughly
competent man must have charge of the arrangements for public meetings. While such an
arrangement is especially necessary in a bye-
election, it is almost as essential at a general
election. If he is assisted by a sub-committee
so much the better.

The central office should be the medium of
communication with all speakers, excepting
those who speak only within the district in
which they live. It should see that every part
of the division is properly served with speakers,
and that a sufficient number of meetings is
arranged for the campaign.

Whether the meetings be few or many it is
desirable that all arrangements should be carried
out with close attention to detail. They should
be fully advertised by handbills, and such other
methods as may be deemed expedient. The
speakers should be advised in good time of the
place and hour of meeting, and it will be the
duty of the central office to check, as far as

possible, any tendency to overcrowd the platforms with speakers. At the same time it is, of course, desirable that the candidate should be well supported by the leading men of each place.

Some of these matters will necessarily be dealt with through the sub-agents, but the central office ought to keep thoroughly in touch with each sub-district, ascertaining the local needs, and supplying them to the best of its ability, while, on the other hand, it should exercise an efficient control of all.

In *Parliamentary* elections there is no limitation, such as exists in the case of committee-rooms, as to the premises upon which public meetings may be held; but care should be taken that no committee business is transacted in connection with meetings held on premises prohibited as committee-rooms. As all payments in connection with public meetings must be made by the election agent or a sub-agent, it is clear that all meetings must be authorized, and the arrangements made by one or other of such agents, otherwise the expenditure incurred would be illegal.

No restrictions as to places where Public Meetings may be held.

The propriety of taking a vote at village meetings is often questioned. It is, however, entirely a matter to be dealt with according to local circumstances. When such a vote is asked for it is seldom that the great bulk of the people present fail to respond.

CANVASSERS AND UNPAID AGENTS.

Canvass-ing. ONE of the most important changes effected by the Corrupt Practices Act of 1883 was the abolition of paid canvassing in connection with elections. It is illegal to employ for payment any person in any capacity, or for any purpose, except such as are authorized by the first and second parts of Schedule I. It is sometimes asserted that a sub-agent, clerk, or messenger, *boná-fide* engaged in such capacity, would not be committing an illegal act by filling up his spare time in visiting or canvassing electors within his district.

It is best, however, to avoid all doubtful practices of the kind, and to rely entirely upon voluntary assistance for the canvass. If a clerk or other paid official spends the whole of his time in canvassing it is obvious that he must either be neglecting the duties he was engaged to perform, or that his services were not required in the capacity in which he was engaged, in which case there would be an evident evasion of the Act. Even if a part only of his time were occupied in canvassing, the same doubt would exist as to the necessity for his employment.

There are many risks to a candidate in connection with canvassing. An authorized canvasser is an agent for whose acts the candidate is responsible. Every precaution should therefore be taken by the election agent and his subordinates to prevent illegal acts on the part of their canvassers. A list of illegal and corrupt practices should be conspicuously displayed in the committee-rooms, and should also be printed in every canvass book, and the attention of canvassers directed thereto. Besides this it is desirable that opportunity should be taken at the committee meetings to impress the members present with their responsibility in these matters. *Canvassers are Agents*

The most common form of error into which volunteer assistants are liable to fall is that of treating. The temptation to discuss political differences over a glass of ale is in many cases very strong, and the consequences are not always apparent. But every canvasser should clearly understand that if he invites an elector to drink at his expense with the object of influencing the elector's mind in favour of a particular candidate or political party he is doing that which is illegal, and may void the election. *Treating by Canvassers.*

Canvassing should not be carried on up to the last moment before the polling. It is an illegal *Canvassing should cease before poll.*

practice, therefore, and a practice which may amount to undue influence, for persons to station themselves in the neighbourhood of a polling-booth and urge voters to vote for a particular candidate. In rural districts this practice is of frequent occurrence, and the offenders are generally employers of labour or other persons of influence. In no case, however, should the election agent or sub-agent allow such persons to go unchecked. The policeman on duty should be requested to put a stop to any interference with the electors, and if he neglect to do so the returning officer or some person in authority under him should be asked to intervene.

Care required in selection of Canvassers. No person should be allowed to take out a canvass-book who is known to have been found guilty of corrupt practices, nor should such a person be allowed to take any part whatever in the election.

The canvass-books should be numbered, and the name of the canvasser with the number of the book taken out by him should be recorded in the district register or some other book provided for the purpose.

Agents. As regards agency, it is one of the most difficult questions in connection with electioneering work. A person may be held to be an agent who has only taken a very slight part in the conduct of the election. What constitutes agency has never yet been exhaustively stated by any judge, and it would, therefore, be hopeless to attempt to define it here; but it would be well to consider every person as an agent of the candidate who has taken any active part in promoting the return of such candidate. Any person, therefore, who has attended committee meetings, who has assisted in the conduct of public meetings, who has introduced the candidate to electors, canvassed on his behalf, or brought up voters on the polling day, should be regarded as an agent, and should be specially warned with reference to illegal acts and their consequences.

BOROUGHS.

GENERAL.

ALTHOUGH the law relating to elections in boroughs is in the main the same as that governing elections in counties, there are some variations of which notice must be taken, and at the risk of considerable repetition they will be dealt with as fully as seems necessary.

The organization of an election campaign in a borough differs materially from that in a county, and this also will be described in detail.

As regards the candidate and the election agent the law is, with one exception, in all respects the same, and it will not be necessary, therefore, to repeat the chapters referring to them. Since the Redistribution Act, however, it is in boroughs only that the question of joint candidature has to be considered, and this subject will be dealt with in a separate chapter.

The following are matters in relation to which there is a difference in the law which must be noted :—

1. In borough elections no sub-agents can be appointed.

2. There is no provision for a central committee-room as such.

3. There may be one committee-room for each 500 electors, or *fraction* of 500.

4. There is no central committee-room staff distinct from the polling district staff; but clerks and messengers may, as in counties, be employed wherever their services are most needed.

5. The maximum scale is lower than in counties.

6. The provision as to carrying voters by sea in certain cases does not apply to boroughs.

7. The question of joint candidature will arise in some instances.

THE ELECTION AGENT.

THE election agent in a borough has a much better opportunity of exercising personal supervision than he has in a county. At the same time there is usually a more active interest in political affairs, and the electors are more accustomed to organized action for a common object than is the case in rural districts. While there are many advantages in this habit of unity, and in the greater activity displayed, they are often modified by the development of personal differences and the formation of cliques. It will be well for the candidate to keep himself clear of all such sectional difficulties; the election agent, however, must acquaint himself with every under-current, and watch its movements as far as possible with the greatest vigilance.

The following matters should receive attention by the election agent in due course, and, where necessary, immediately after his appointment:— *Matters needing Election Agent's attention.*

1. The printing and circulation of the candidate's address.

2. The engagement of suitable committee-rooms in the various polling districts.

3. The appointment of clerks and messengers.

4. The preparation of canvass books and district registers.

5. The formation of an election committee and sub-committees.

6. The organization of the ward or polling district committees.

7. The arrangement of a plan of public meetings to cover the borough, and the securing of the necessary rooms in which to hold such meetings.

8. The filling up of nomination papers.

9. The appointment of polling or personation agents, and of counting agents.

10. The giving of notice to the returning officer—

  (*a*) By the candidate, of the appointment of an election agent and of the address of his office ;

  (*b*) By the election agent, of the appointment of personation agents and counting agents.

11. The taking of the declaration of secrecy by the candidate, by the election agent, and by the personation and counting agents.

12. The payment of claims, and making of return and declaration of election expenses within the prescribed time.

The issuing of the candidate's address to the electors and the preparation of the canvass books, etc., are matters which demand the immediate attention of the election agent. In boroughs the register is generally made up in street order, and the task of preparing canvass books is, therefore, much more simple than in counties. It is recommended that not more than twenty or twenty-five names should be put in each book. No time should be lost before issuing the books to the ward committees.

JOINT CANDIDATURE.

IT would appear that joint candidature is not assumed to exist prior to such period as the candidates, in view of an impending election, enter into certain contracts or engagements which in themselves establish joint candidature. Up to this time each candidate is apparently liable only for his own acts and for those of his personal agents or supporters, provided he had no knowledge at the time of entering upon the joint candidature of any corrupt or illegal practices previously committed by or on behalf of the other party to the coalition.

Candidates are treated as joint who either —

Who are Joint Candidates.

(*a*) Appoint the same election agents ;

(*b*) Hire or use the same committee-rooms by themselves or any agent ;

(*c*) Employ the same sub-agents, clerks, messengers, or polling agents ;

(*d*) Publish a joint address, or joint circular or notice.

In cases (*b*) and (*c*) the candidature will not be deemed joint if the hire or employment be accidental or trivial. The joint candidature may be entered upon or dissolved at any time.

ELECTION EXPENSES.

THE maximum scale in boroughs, as in counties, is exclusive of the returning officer's charges, and of the candidate's personal expenses. There is no provision in the case of boroughs for conveying voters by sea.

The following is the scale in England and Wales :—

BOROUGHS.

Constituency.	For one Candidate.	For two Joint Candidates.
Not exceeding—	£	£
2,000 electors	350	525
3,000 ,,	380	570
4,000 ,,	410	615
5,000 ,,	440	660
6,000 ,	470	705
7,000 ,,	500	750
8,000 .,	530	795
9,000 ,,	560	840
10,000 ,,	590	885
11,000 ,,	620	930
12,000 ,,	650	975
13,000 ,,	680	1,020
14,000 ,,	710	1,065
15,000 ,,	740	1,110

and so on, adding £30 for every complete 1,000 electors in the case of single candidates, and £45 for every complete 1,000 electors in the

I

case of two joint candidates. Two joint candidates may spend *one-and-a-half times as much,* and three joint candidates *twice as much* as a single candidate.

Responsibilities of Candidates and Agents, in connection with Expenses. In other respects the same duties and responsibilities are cast upon candidates and agents in boroughs as in counties, *i.e.* :—

1. The candidate (or candidates) must deliver to the election agent within fourteen days of the day of election a statement of the amount of personal expenses paid by himself, and must examine the accounts and make the declaration as to election expenses.

2. (*a*) The election agent must collect all outstanding accounts (including his own claim) within fourteen days after the day on which the candidates returned are declared elected, excepting only the returning officer's claim, which must be received within twenty-one days after the day on which the return is made.

(*b*) Must pay all claims within twenty-eight days of the date on which the result of the election is declared.

(*c*) Must give particulars and file a receipt for all sums amounting to 40s. and upwards.

(*d*) Must make the declaration as to election expenses.

(*e*) Must transmit within thirty-five days to the returning officer the return and declaration respecting election expenses.

Any claim not paid within the stipulated time must be returned as a disputed claim.

Any violation of the rules laid down by the Act is an illegal practice, and may render the election void, and failure to transmit the return and declarations within the time named also disables the candidate from sitting or voting as Member in the House of Commons under a penalty of £100 for every day on which he so sits and votes.

A false declaration renders the person making it liable to indictment for perjury, and to the penalty for that offence, namely, seven years' penal servitude.

COMMITTEE-ROOMS.

Prohibited Premises. IN boroughs, as in counties, committee-rooms are prohibited on the following premises :—

Premises licensed for the sale, wholesale or retail, of intoxicating liquors ; or on which intoxicating liquors *or refreshments of any kind, whether food or drink*, are supplied for consumption on the premises.

[An exception is made in favour of permanent political clubs, but it is best, as a rule, to avoid establishing committee-rooms in a club. The reasons are now pretty generally understood, and it is unnecessary to repeat them here.]

The premises which are prohibited, therefore, may be taken to include :—

Public-houses and hotels ;

Grocers' and other shops having licenses ;

The premises of brewers, wine and spirit merchants ;

Coffee and tea houses ; and certain

Confectioners' shops where refreshments are supplied for consumption on the premises.

Any part of such premises may, however, be used for a committee-room if such part is ordinarily let for chambers, offices, etc., *and provided it has a separate entrance and no direct communication with any part where liquor is sold or refreshments supplied.*

It is, however, very unusual for such conditions to exist, and it is doubtful whether the temporary closing and sealing of any passage or other means of communication generally existing would meet the requirements of the Act.

An agent will, therefore, be well advised if he avoid all risks in this matter.

Public elementary schools are also in the list of places prohibited.

It must be borne in mind that in the case of borough elections the Act makes no provision for a central committee-room : hence the election agent must use one of his ward or polling district committee-rooms for his central office, and he must take care that there is sufficient room in the premises to accommodate his own staff as well as that of the polling district.

Number of Committee-rooms which may be hired.

The number of committee-rooms for which payment may be made is as follows :—

One committee-room in any case, and if there are more than 500 electors on the register one extra committee-room for each additional 500 or *fraction* of 500.

	Electors.	No. of Committee-rooms.

Thus, in a borough or division

of a borough having 500 (or less) 1

501 to 1,000 2

1,001 to 1,500 3

1,501 to 2,000 4

and so on.

There is no limit to the number of rooms which may be used, provided —

(*a*) That no payment or promise of payment is made for any room in excess of the legal number.

(*b*) That they are not on prohibited premises.

Number required. The number of committee-rooms required will, of course, vary according to the size of the borough. In the smaller constituencies two or three may be sufficient for all purposes; but in bigger places it will be necessary to arrange for a greater number.

There should be at least one committee-room in each ward; and it is a good plan in boroughs of the largest size, where a single ward will often contain 4,000 or 5,000 electors, to open a room in every polling district for an hour or two each evening prior to the day of election, in order that electors who are at work late, and, perhaps, have neither time nor inclination to visit the ward committee-room, may have a place within easy reach of home where they may call to give or receive information. There should be a complete register for the borough in every ward committee-room, and the list of electors for the polling district in each polling district committee-room.

Committee-rooms must be hired by the election agent, and the following form may be used :—

MEMORANDUM OF AGREE-MENT FOR HIRE OF COM-MITTEE-ROOM.

I . . . agree to let to . . . agent for . . . at the Parliamentary election for the . . . division of the . . . of . . . the room or premises described in the memorandum signed by the said agent and now handed to me, for the consideration and on the conditions named therein. Price: . . . inclusive of firing, lighting, and cleaning. . . . Dated this . . . day of . . . 189 . (Signed) . . .

MEMORANDUM OF AGREE-MENT FOR HIRE OF COM-MITTEE-ROOM.

I . . . election agent for . . . a candidate in the Parliamentary election now being held for the . . . Division of the . . . of . . . hereby agree to hire . . . for use as a committee-room for the said candidate from the present day until the declaration of the poll, and I agree to pay for the same the sum of £ . . . which sum shall include the cost of firing, lighting, and cleaning for the said room or premises. Dated this . . . day of . . . 189 . (Signed) . .

ELECTION COMMITTEES.

MOST of what has been said with reference to election committees in counties applies with at least equal force to the same bodies in boroughs. The borough election committee will, however, be able to meet more often and with less waste of time than the county committee. It is desirable that it should meet frequently to receive reports from the different wards, to take measures for strengthening weak places, and to devise methods of counteracting the tactics of opponents.

The committee should not be too large a body—two representatives from each of the wards would be sufficient, and in order that any person whose help would be valuable could afterwards be invited to join, power might be taken to add a limited number to the committee.

How they should be constituted. It is particularly necessary in boroughs to bear in mind that the election committee should consist only of the most trusted and influential men in the party. Although no doubt the bulk of the committee would be selected from the executive of the party association, it is not necessary, and it is indeed undesirable that it should be limited to such members. It has to be borne in mind that the doctrine of agency may be extended almost indefinitely, and that, consequently, if an election committee consisted exclusively of the members of one association, every person belonging to that association might be reasonably held to be an agent of the candidate.

It would appear, therefore, that the safer plan is so to constitute the election committee that it shall represent every section of the electorate, while it is in itself a body entirely independent of any other organization.

Having appointed a chairman and secretary, the committee would turn its attention to the organization of the wards. In co-operation with the election agent, it should inquire into the strength and resources of the various local committees, their methods of working, and their state of preparedness. *Their duties and responsibilities.*

Sub-committees to assist in arranging for meetings, speakers, literature, etc., may be appointed, and if necessary a small committee to detect corrupt practices may be formed. In all cases the maximum number on a sub-committee should be three.

As soon as the canvass books are written up and ready for distribution the ward committees should be convened. There is sometimes a *Ward Committees.*

difference of opinion as to who should convene them. It is submitted that the election agent is the proper person to do this, mainly for the reason that he alone has legal authority to incur the necessary expenditure ; but also because he is responsible for the acts of every person summoned to any committee meetings on behalf of the candidate he represents. The responsibility thus resting upon him is so great that he ought to guard jealously his right to control the appointment of "agents," whether they be paid or unpaid. He should, in company with the chairman and secretary of the election committee, carefully examine the lists of persons whom it is proposed to invite to join the ward or district committees, and under no circumstances should an invitation be allowed to go out to any person about whose loyalty or antecedents there is any shadow of doubt. The election agent should keep the lists of the ward committees in his own possession, and the notices summoning meetings of the committees should all bear his name and be sent out from his office.

Precau-
tions to
be taken. Care should also be taken to keep a record of the names of those attending the committee meetings, and any person attending uninvited should be asked to retire, unless it is considered desirable to add his name to the committee.

Every member of the central and district committees should receive a memorandum of illegal and corrupt practices and the penalties attending them.

The election agent should endeavour to attend the *first* meeting of each ward committee, and as far as possible all subsequent formal meetings, which need not, of course, be very frequent. At the first meeting he should explain in detail to the members his plan of operations and the part he desires the committee to take in carrying it out. He should take special pains to impress the members with their responsibility as agents of the candidate, and the obligation resting upon every individual to avoid doing anything himself which may imperil the election, and also, as far as he can, to prevent others from committing illegal acts.

Agent and Candidate to attend Ward Meetings.

It is very desirable that the candidate should also attend the committee meetings whenever his other engagements leave him an opportunity. His presence and a few words of encouragement will stimulate the workers to renewed exertions.

In giving out the canvass books it is very important to keep an accurate record of the name and address of each canvasser and of the number of the book he takes. There should be space in the district registers for such entries; and the canvasser's name should also be written on the canvass book itself.

Record of Canvasser's name to be kept.

The clerk in charge of the ward committee-room, or some other person, should take a report of the canvass every evening from those holding the books. On no account should any canvasser be allowed to keep a book in his possession without reporting what he has done. If he fails to put in an appearance for two consecutive evenings, he should be looked up without hesitation, and if he can offer no satisfactory explanation, or if he has done no work, the book should be demanded of him and given to someone else, or a new book made out and put in the hands of a more diligent worker.

Daily Report of Canvass to be made. A daily report of the canvass should be made to the election agent.

All removals should be entered up on the sheets provided for the purpose, and reported daily to the election agent; and a special canvass should be made of removals *into* the ward reported from the central office.

Poll Cards. If the poll cards are to be sent out from the district committee-room, a set of envelopes should be addressed as early as possible in the contest, and corrections of addresses made from time to time as required. If the cards are to be sent from the central office, this work must of course be done there; and as, in this case, they would probably be sent through the post, the election agent should arrange beforehand with the post-office officials when to hand them in. Two days before the opening of the poll may be considered as the proper time for posting in boroughs, and by giving notice to the postmaster of his intention to post on a certain date, the agent will not only assist the officials, but will do much to secure the prompt and efficient delivery of the cards.

Where it is desired that the district committees shall arrange for the delivery of the cards by hand, it will be essential that they should be able to begin the distribution at least two days before the poll opens. A full meeting of the whole of the ward committees should therefore be held not less than three days before the day of election, when the plan of distribution should be arranged, and each member should receive his proportion of cards and enclosures, with instructions to commence delivery on the following evening, and to finish absolutely on the evening before the opening of the poll.

Of the merits of the different methods of distribution here discussed, the local committees will be in the best position to judge, and they will naturally be guided by circumstances in deciding which course it will be most advantageous to adopt ; but, generally speaking, it is deemed advisable to send the cards by post.

The clerk in charge of the ward must see that the personation agent's list is marked up in good time, and every effort should be made to ensure accuracy in the notes. *Final Preparations for Poll.*

He must also have written up canvassing cards for the election day, containing the names of all electors who have promised their vote.

Before the polling day, and usually on the eve of the poll, the whole of the committees should be called together in their several wards to receive final instructions as to their duties. It may not be possible for the election agent to attend all these meetings, and he should therefore arrange for some other competent person to share the task with him. At these meetings the final report of the canvass should be entered in the district registers, and the canvass books called in. It is the usual, and ought to be the invariable, plan to open a committee-room in every polling district on the day of the poll. It will, therefore, be necessary to appoint at least one person to take charge of each room, and be responsible for the polling of the promises in that district. The canvassers must be informed of the situation of the room and the time they are expected to be present, which should not be less than half-an-hour before the opening of the poll. Vehicles should also be allotted, and a list handed to the clerks.

It will not, of course, be possible for the election agent to remain while all these details are gone into. He should therefore open the proceedings by whatever words of encouragement the circumstances will admit of, give such instructions as he deems necessary, and proceed to the other meetings.

Committee-room Stationery.

At each ward committee-room he should leave a parcel containing the following lists and stationery :—

A copy of the register for the whole borough, to be kept at the ward committee-room.

A copy of the register of electors in each polling district in the ward.

Extra canvassing cards (blank).

Extra poll cards (blank).

Lists of vehicles at command of the district committee-rooms.

Numbers for carriages.

Lists of authorized canvassers and volunteer helpers.

Lists of corrupt and illegal practices and penalties for display in committee-room.

Instructions to personation agents.

Foolscap paper.

Note paper and envelopes.

Blotting paper.

Pens, pencils, and ink.

Red and blue pencils.

Paper fasteners.

Perforated slips for checkers.

On the polling day the district committees On Day should assemble at their respective committee- Poll. rooms at 7.30. The secretary, or other person in charge of the room, should take the names of all in attendance, and then proceed to distribute the "fetching up cards." The outside carriage superintendent will meanwhile see that the vehicles as they arrive are checked off on his list, and that each carriage has a number attached. If there are any voters to be fetched so early, he will also see that this is attended to.

If the personation agents have not already received the marked lists, these must, of course,

be delivered now. It will be necessary, in any
case, for the committee-room superintendent to
ascertain whether the personation agent is in his
place at eight o'clock ; if he is not, inquiry as to
his whereabouts should immediately be made.

Voters who have polled must be marked off in
the district register, and at the close of the poll
this book, together with other books and documents, must be made up into a parcel and sent
to the election agent.

CANVASSERS AND UNPAID AGENTS.

THE same rules apply in boroughs as in counties. Principal points to observe. It is, therefore, unnecessary to repeat all that has been said on the subject, but it may be useful to recapitulate the principal points to be observed.

1. No canvasser may be engaged for payment or promise of payment.

2. No person should be allowed to take out a canvass book who is known to have been found guilty of corrupt practices, nor should such a person be allowed to take any part whatever in the election.

3. The canvass books should be numbered, and the name of the canvasser with the number of the book taken out by him should be recorded in the district register or some other book provided for the purpose.

4. An authorized canvasser is an agent for whose acts the candidate is respon-

K

sible. Every precaution should therefore be taken by the election agent
and his subordinates to prevent illega
acts on the part of their canvassers.

5. Canvassing should not be carried on up to
the last moment before the polling.
It is an illegal practice, therefore,
and a practice which may amount to
undue influence, for persons to station
themselves in the neighbourhood of
a polling-booth and urge voters to
vote for a particular candidate.

6. A list of illegal and corrupt practices
should be conspicuously displayed in
the committee-rooms, and should also
be printed in every canvass book,
and the attention of canvassers
directed thereto.

CLERKS.

THE number of clerks who may be employed for payment in a borough election is—

		Electors.	No. of Clerks.
In a borough having		500 (or less) ...	1
,,	,,	501 to 1,000 ...	2
,,	,,	1,001 to 1,500	3
,,	,,	1,501 to 2,000 ...	4

and so on, adding one clerk for every 500 electors, or fraction of 500.

The election agent will, as a rule, require in his office the following staff :— Staff required at Central Office.

One clerk to assist with the correspondence, and to keep a record of expenses.

One clerk to superintend arrangements for public meetings.

One clerk to deal with removals.

One clerk to arrange for vehicles on the polling day, and to distribute to the ward committee-rooms the literature used during the election.

The expenses clerk should keep a daily record of money paid and of orders given. He should

see that an invoice is received with all goods
delivered, and should endeavour to keep an
accurate account of the expenditure incurred
from day to day.

**Public
Meetings.**
The meetings clerk should immediately on his
appointment consult with the ward committees
as to the meetings to be held, and should ascertain what rooms are available, the dates on
which they are free, and the terms on which they
may be engaged. Having drawn up a scheme
of meetings for a week or so in advance, he
should at once obtain from the election agent a
written order for every room wanted, and should
forthwith secure the places. He will then have
to arrange with the election agent for the
speakers to attend each meeting, and these
having been decided upon he should at once get
the necessary handbills printed and forwarded to
the ward committee-rooms for distribution. If
posters are used in addition, they will, of course,
be sent to the ordinary bill-poster or advertising
agent.

Every advertisement of a meeting should give
the following particulars :—

> (*a*.) The place where the meeting will be
> held.
> (*b*.) The street or road in which the room is
> situated.
> (*c*.) The date (stating the day of the week
> as well as the day of the month).
> (*d*.) The time of beginning.

(c.) The names of the chairman and
principal speakers.

(f.) A bold announcement of the name of
the candidate.

A proof of every bill and poster should be
examined, and particular care must be taken that
it bears the name and address of the printer and
publisher.

Everyone who is expected to speak at a
meeting should be advised early and fully, and if
he is coming from a distance the train by which
he ought to travel should be stated, and someone
should be appointed to meet that train on its
arrival.

There is no limitation, such as exists in the
case of committee-rooms, as to the premises
upon which public meetings may be held; but
care should be taken that no committee business
is transacted in connection with meetings held on
premises prohibited as committee-rooms. As all
payments in connection with public meetings
must be made by the election agent, it is clear
that all meetings must be authorized by him,
otherwise the expenditure incurred would be
illegal.

The removals clerk in a borough will usually **Removals.**
have a heavy task. Very often the removals will
amount to a fifth, or even a fourth of the whole
electorate. The best system of dealing with them
is in the main the same as that already described
in connection with county removals, but the

matter is of such importance that it may be well to repeat the main features of the plan.

The work of following up removals ought to be well in hand before the beginning of the contest. Where this is the case each member of a Polling District Committee will have been furnished with a little book containing twenty or thirty slips with blank spaces as follows :—

No. 1.—REMOVALS TRACED PREVIOUS TO FLECTION.

. . . Polling District. Name of outgoing tenant . . . Removed from . . . to . . . Date of Removal . . . Politics . . . Name of incoming tenant . . . Removed from . . . to . . . Date of Removal . . . Politics . . . Signed . . . Canvasser.

The particulars will have been reported at the periodical meetings of the committees, and entered up in books kept for the purpose at the central office.

Assuming, however, that such preparations have not been made, it will be necessary to collect information with the utmost possible despatch.

Two classes of Removals.

Removals may be divided into two classes :—

(1) Those who have removed from one polling district to another within the same borough or division of a borough; and

(2) Those who have removed outside the borough or division altogether.

It will simplify the work if the first class is dealt with by the ward or district clerks themselves communicating one with another, but all voters coming in the second should be dealt with at the central committee-room.

The canvassers' reports will afford a large amount of information with reference to removals, and clerks in charge of committee-rooms should make a daily return of all instances discovered. The returns through the Dead Letter Office when the candidate's address has been posted to the electors will also afford much valuable information.

As the Post-Office returns come in they should be carefully sorted over, and particulars forwarded to the officials in whose districts the voter's qualification exists with the following note and form :—

No. 2.—REMOVALS—POST-OFFICE RETURNS.

Parliamentary Election for the . . . Division of the Borough of . . . Central Committee Room . . . 189 . The Election Address sent to the undermentioned Electors has been returned by the Post-office authorities marked " Left." Kindly have a special canvass made with the object of ascertaining whether any error has been made by the Post-office officials, and of finding out as far as may be possible where the removed voters are now residing.

Reg. No.	Name.	Removed from.	To.

Where the voter's new address has been ascertained, and it is found to be outside the Parliamentary Division, the names should at once be forwarded to the party agents in the district to which the voters have removed.

The following form may be used :—

No. 3.—REMOVALS.

Parliamentary Election for the . . . Division of the Borough of . . .
To . . .

Central Committee-room.

. . .
. . .

The undermentioned persons having a qualification in this Division are reported as having removed into your district. I should be greatly obliged if you would have them canvassed and any information you are able to obtain as to the present address, politics, and intentions of the voter marked up on this form, which should be returned to me at the earliest possible date.

No. on Reg.	Name of Elector.	Address on Register.	Removed to.	Politics.		Remarks. (a) Whether Elector intends to vote. (b) Whether he desires to be met at station. (c) Time of his arrival, etc., etc., etc.
				L.	C.	

Where the voter's new address is within the same Parliamentary Borough or Division of a Borough particulars should be forwarded to the ward or district clerk *from whose district the voter has removed*, and he will institute the necessary inquiries on a similar form.

Traced Removals. The removals clerk will, of course, keep a record of all replies received to his inquiries; and will also forward to the ward or district clerks from whose districts the voters have removed all information he is able to get concerning them. A traced removals form is shown below:—

Parliamentary Election for the . . . Division of the . . . of . . . 189 .
No. 4.—TRACED REMOVALS.—POLLING DISTRICT . . .

Reg. No.	Name.	Politics.		Removed from.	Present Address.	Remarks.
		L.	C.			

He must also arrange with the party agents in

the various Divisions where removed voters are residing, that on the polling day the said voters shall be canvassed in the same way as though they were still living within the constituency where they are entitled to vote. On the polling day he should keep up communications with the various agents until he learns that every voter is known to be on his way to the polling booth, or that from some unpreventable cause he is absolutely unable to record his vote.

As regards removals from one polling district to another within the same Parliamentary Borough or Division, with which it is suggested the ward or district clerks should deal direct between themselves, the following is a sketch of the plan that should be adopted :— *Removals within the same Borough.*

In most cases of removal reported the canvassers will have been able to make some statement as to the place where the voter has gone to reside. It will then be the business of the clerk to see that the name of the voter is at once sent on to the clerk within whose district the voter now lives, with a request that he shall be canvassed and reported on (see Removals Form No. 3). When no information as to the new address is forthcoming at first the name should be sent to every ward or district clerk within the Parliamentary Borough or Division with a request that full inquiry shall be made as to whether such a person has come to reside in his district. At the same time, of course, no effort should be spared to find out some neighbour who can give information as to where the removed voter has gone.

Where a canvass thus organized is thoroughly carried out almost every removal can be traced; any voter not found should be specially marked on the personation agent's list, and if he presents himself to vote the presiding officer should be asked to put the usual questions to him.

In the case of removals reported upon as pledged to vote in favour of the candidate in whose interest he has been canvassed, pains should be taken to ascertain whether it is necessary to convey him to the poll; and if so, *the ward or district clerk into whose district he has removed* should, generally speaking, undertake the responsibility of sending a vehicle to take him to the polling place and bring him back again.

Of course it will be borne in mind that no railway, 'bus, or tram fares may be paid, and that no horse or vehicle ordinarily let for hire may be employed to convey voters to the poll.

Convey-
ances.

The vehicles clerk or superintendent should, without delay, send out a letter to every person in the neighbourhood who is at all likely to help on the polling day by the loan of a horse and conveyance of any kind, asking whether a vehicle can be lent, and, if so, what kind it will be. He must remember that the Corrupt Practices Act makes it illegal —

(a) To make any payment or contract for payment before, during, or after an election on account of the conveyance of voters to or from the poll.

(b) To " let, lend, or employ," or to " hire, borrow, or use," for conveying electors to the poll, any *carriage, horse or other animal* ordinarily kept or used for the purpose of letting out for hire.—C. P. A., Sec. 14.

It is therefore illegal to *use* for the conveyance of voters to the poll any horse or carriage ordinarily let out for hire by any person, even if such horse or carriage is offered gratuitously by the owner.

There is nothing, however, to prevent any person owning a vehicle or an animal which is *not* ordinarily let out for hire, lending such vehicle or animal for use on the polling day, provided, of course, that no payment or promise of payment is made.

Having ascertained what carriages will be available, he should, a day or two before the election, consult with the agent and the committee as to the disposal of them. The allotment having been made, the ward or district clerks should be informed what vehicles they may expect on the polling day, and the owners of the conveyances should also be told the address of the committee-room to which their vehicles are to be sent, the name of the person in charge, and the time at

Allotment to Polling Districts.

which they should arrive. It would be well also to send to each committee-room some such instructions as the following :—

Instructions for Management of Vehicles on Day of Poll.

At each committee-room there should be one person whose sole duty it will be to regulate the service from that committee-room, and no one should be allowed to take away a carriage without instructions are given by that person.

The clerk in charge of the committee-room should extract from his district register particulars as to those electors who have expressed a desire for a carriage to be sent for them. These particulars should be put on slips and arranged on an ordinary bill file in time order. Thus—those who are to be fetched at eight o'clock would come first, half-past eight following in order, and so on. The slips should be passed out at the proper time to the vehicle superintendent, who should then despatch a carriage for the voter, the driver or a canvasser accompanying him being requested to report at the committee-room when the elector has polled. Should the voter not keep his appointment the slip should be passed back into the committee-room and placed on another file, to be dealt with at a fitting opportunity later in the day.

The carriage superintendent should be carefully instructed as to polling removals from other districts.

The main points to be insisted upon are —

1. That the vehicles shall be under the control of the polling district clerk *in* the committee-room, and of the carriage superintendent outside the committee-room.

2. That voters known to require fetching at stated times shall receive first attention ; and

3 That no person shall be allowed to take vehicles away without an order from the carriage superintendent.

There is usually a slack time on election day, and advantage should be taken of this to rest the horses in view of the heavy demands made on their strength during the latter part of the day.

The carriage clerk at the central office previously to the polling day will generally have some time at his disposal, and he should therefore be required to apportion the literature received at the office and see that it is despatched to the various district committee-rooms. He should be assisted by one of the messengers as packer.

Distribution of Literature.

An experienced clerk should be put in charge
at every ward committee-room, and he should
be held responsible for the proper canvass of his
ward, the arrangements in connection with
public meetings, and for all other details in connection with the working of the election both
before and on the day of the poll.

Upon the clerks in charge of ward or district
committee-rooms will devolve many of the duties
performed by sub-agents in counties, although
they are not invested by law with precisely the
same responsibility. They must carry out the
instructions of the election agent, and they must
see that all details are carried out in accordance
with the requirements of the law. They should,
of course, be careful to work in harmony with
the local committees.

They should take care that all the matters
alluded to in the chapter on election committees
are duly attended to. It will be their duty to
make a daily return of the canvass to the election
agent. As they will be called upon to make
many small payments in connection with the
election, they should take care to obtain a written
authority from the election agent to expend a
specified sum on account of petty expenses. A
strict account of all such expenditure must be
kept and particulars furnished in due time to the
election agent, together with receipts for all
sums of 40s. and upwards.

MESSENGERS.

THE duties of messengers need no special description.

The same number of messengers as of clerks may be employed.

PERSONATION AND COUNTING AGENTS.

THE same rules as in counties apply to these agents in boroughs, and reference should be made to the chapters on the subject in the first part of this manual.

NOMINATION.

PRECISELY the same rules must be observed as in counties. These have already been described in the first part of the manual, p. 80.

APPENDIX.

PROHIBITED VOTING.

It is an offence—

    (*a*) For any prohibited person to vote ;

    (*b*) To induce or procure any prohibited person to vote.

Persons "prohibited from voting" are persons otherwise capable of voting, and who would be entitled to vote, were they not disqualified by statute. The rule, therefore, does not apply to persons who are prohibited from voting by the common law of Parliament. For example, if a peer, or a woman votes, no illegal practice is committed within the meaning of the Corrupt Practices Act.

The following persons are prohibited by statute from voting in England and Wales :—

1. Infants—*i.e.*, persons who have not completed their 21st year on the polling day.

2. Persons convicted of treason or felony, who have not been pardoned, and whose term of punishment has not expired.

3. Electors who, within six months of the election, have been retained, hired, or employed for reward, for all or any of the purposes of the election, by, or on behalf of, any candidate at such election, as agent, clerk, messenger, or in other like employment.

4. Persons guilty of any corrupt or illegal practice, or of illegal employment, payment, or hiring at an election,

may not vote at that election, and their votes are void.

5. Persons who have become incapable of voting by reason of offences at former elections, for which they have been convicted or reported. may not vote at any election while such incapacity lasts.

[Persons convicted of corrupt practices are incapable of voting for *seven years ;* persons convicted of illegal practices are incapable of voting for *five years* from the date of conviction.

Persons reported as having been guilty of corrupt or illegal practices, *although receiving a certificate of indemnity,* are subject to the same incapacity as if they had been convicted of the offence at the date of the election.]

6. Returning officers may not vote except in case of an equality of votes.

Note.—The Police Disabilities Removal Act, 1887, has removed the prohibition formerly existing in the case of police constables, and special provision is made by Clause 2 to enable constables on duty at a distance from the polling station at which their qualification entitles them to vote, to record their votes at any booth in the electoral division.

Clauses 2 and 3 of this Act are given on p. 149.

The following persons are incapacitated from voting at Parliamentary elections, and their votes may be refused by the presiding officer :—

Aliens.

Women.

Peers.

Idiots.

Lunatics.
[The vote of a lunatic given in a lucid interval is good.]
Drunkards.

POLICE DISABILITIES REMOVAL ACT, 1887.

50 Vict., Sess. 2, Chapter 9.

Clause 2. Where a constable is, or is likely to be, on the day of any election sent or employed in the discharge of his duty so as to prevent him voting at the polling booth or station at which he would otherwise be entitled by law to vote, the following enactments shall have effect :— *Constable on duty to be entitled to Vote at any Polling Station.*

(1.) Such constable may, at any time within seven days before the election, apply to the chief constable for a certificate, and the chief constable shall thereupon give a certificate under his hand, stating the name of the constable, his number in the police force, his number and description on the register of voters, and the fact that he is so sent or employed ;

(2.) The presiding officer at any polling booth or station shall, on production by such constable of the said certificate, allow him to vote at that booth or station, and shall forthwith cancel the said certificate, and deal with the same in like manner as the counterfoils of voting papers are directed by law to be dealt with ;

(3.) No such constable shall, under this section, be entitled to vote at any election at which he would not, but for this section, be entitled to vote, nor more than once in any election, and if he so votes, or attempts to vote, he shall be subject to all the penalties imposed by law on a person personating or attempting to personate a voter at such election ;

(4.) In this section —

    (a.) " Constable " includes any person belonging to a police force ;

    (b.) " Chief constable " includes an assistant chief constable, a commissioner or assistant commissioner of police, a head constable, and any other person for the time being in command of a police force, or acting in that capacity ;

(*c.*) "Register of voters" has the same meaning as in the Ballot Act, 1872.

Registration in case of temporary absence of Police Officer on duty.

3. A person otherwise entitled to be registered as a voter at parliamentary elections in respect of the occupation of a dwelling-house shall be deemed an inhabitant occupier thereof as tenant notwithstanding his temporary absence therefrom in the execution of duty as a police officer during a part of the qualifying period, not exceeding four consecutive months.

CORRUPT AND ILLEGAL PRACTICES PREVENTION ACT, 1883.

46 and 47 Vict., Chapter 51.

Corrupt Practices.

What is Treating ?

1. Whereas under section four of the Corrupt Practices Prevention Act, 1854, persons other than candidates at parliamentary elections are not liable to any punishment for treating, and it is expedient to make such persons liable ; be it therefore enacted in substitution for the said section four as follows :—

(1.) Any person who corruptly by himself or by any other person, either before, during, or after an election, directly or indirectly gives or provides, or pays wholly or in part the expense of giving or providing, any meat drink entertainment or provision to or for any person, for the purpose of corruptly influencing that person or any other person to give or refrain from giving his vote at the election, or on account of such person or any other person having voted or refrained from voting, or being about to vote or refrain from voting at such election, shall be guilty of treating.

(2.) And every elector who corruptly accepts or takes any such meat drink entertainment or provision shall also be guilty of treating.

2. Every person who shall directly or indirectly, by himself or by any other person on his behalf, make use of or threaten to make use of any force, violence, or restraint, or inflict or threaten to inflict, by himself or by any other person, any temporal or spiritual injury, damage, harm, or loss upon or against any person in order to induce or compel such person to vote or refrain from voting, or on account of such person having voted or refrained from voting at any election, or who shall by abduction, duress, or any fraudulent device or contrivance impede or prevent the free exercise of the franchise of any elector, or shall thereby compel, induce, or prevail upon any elector either to give or to refrain from giving his vote at any election, shall be guilty of undue influence. *What is Undue Influence?*

3. The expression "corrupt practice" as used in this Act means any of the following offences, namely, treating and undue influence, as defined by this Act, and bribery, and personation, as defined by the enactments set forth in Part III. of the Third Schedule to this Act, and aiding, abetting, counselling, and procuring the commission of the offence of personation, and every offence which is a corrupt practice within the meaning of this Act shall be a corrupt practice within the meaning of the Parliamentary Elections Act, 1868. *What is Corrupt Practice?*

4. Where upon the trial of an election petition respecting an election for a county or borough the election court, by the report made to the Speaker in pursuance of section eleven of the Parliamentary Elections Act, 1868, reports that any corrupt practice other than treating or undue influence has been proved to have been committed in reference to such *Punishment of Candidate found on Election Petition guilty personally of Corrupt Practices.*

election by or with the knowledge and consent of any candidate at such election, or that the offence of treating or undue influence has been proved to have been committed in reference to such election by any candidate at such election, that candidate shall not be capable of ever being elected to or sitting in the House of Commons for the said county or borough, and if he has been elected his election shall be void ; and he shall further be subject to the same incapacities as if at the date of the said report he had been convicted on an indictment of a corrupt practice.

Punishment of Candidate found on Election Petition guilty by Agents of Corrupt Practices. **5.** Upon the trial of an election petition respecting an election for a county or borough, in which a charge is made of any corrupt practice having been committed in reference to such election, the election court shall report in writing to the Speaker whether any of the candidates at such election has been guilty by his agents of any corrupt practice in reference to such election ; and if the report is that any candidate at such election has been guilty by his agents of any corrupt practice in reference to such election, that candidate shall not be capable of being elected to or sitting in the House of Commons for such county or borough for seven years after the date of the report. and if he has been elected his election shall be void.

Punishment of person convicted on indictment of Corrupt Practices. **6.** (1.) A person who commits any corrupt practice other than personation, or aiding, abetting, counselling, or procuring the commission of the offence of personation, shall be guilty of a misdemeanor, and on conviction on indictment shall be liable to be imprisoned, with or without hard labour, for a term not exceeding one year, or to be fined any sum not exceeding two hundred pounds.

(2.) A person who commits the offence of personation, or of aiding, abetting, counselling, or procuring the commission of that offence, shall be guilty of felony, and any person con-

victed thereof on indictment shall be punished by imprisonment for a term not exceeding two years, together with hard
labour.

(3.) A person who is convicted on indictment of any
corrupt practice shall (in addition to any punishment as
above provided) be not capable during a period of seven years
from the date of his conviction :

- *a*.) of being registered as an elector or voting at any
  election in the United Kingdom, whether it be a
  parliamentary election or an election for any public
  office within the meaning of this Act ; or
- (*b*.) of holding any public or judicial office within the
  meaning of this Act, and if he holds any such office
  the office shall be vacated.

(4.) Any person so convicted of a corrupt practice in
reference to any election shall also be incapable of being
elected to and of sitting in the House of Commons during
the seven years next after the date of his conviction, and if
at that date he has been elected to the House of Commons
his election shall be vacated from the time of such conviction.

Illegal Practices.

7. (1.) No payment or contract for payment shall, for
the purpose of promoting or procuring the election of a
candidate at any election, be made — [*Certain expenditure to be Illegal Practice.*]

- (*a*.) on account of the conveyance of electors to or from
  the poll, whether for the hiring of horses or carriages,
  or for railway fares, or otherwise; or
- (*b*.) to an elector on account of the use of any house,
  land, building, or premises for the exhibition of any
  address, bill, or notice, or on account of the exhibition of any address, bill, or notice ; or

(*c.*) on account of any committee-room in excess of the number allowed by the first schedule to this Act.

(2.) Subject to such exception as may be allowed in pursuance of this Act, if any payment or contract for payment is knowingly made in contravention of this section either before, during, or after an election, the person making such payment or contract shall be guilty of an illegal practice, and any person receiving such payment or being a party to any such contract, knowing the same to be in contravention of this Act, shall also be guilty of an illegal practice.

(3.) Provided that where it is the ordinary business of an elector as an advertising agent to exhibit for payment bills and advertisements, a payment to or contract with such elector, if made in the ordinary course of business, shall not be deemed to be an illegal practice within the meaning of this section.

Expense in excess of maximum to be Illegal Practice. **8.** (1.) Subject to such exception as may be allowed in pursuance of this Act, no sum shall be paid and no expense shall be incurred by a candidate at an election or his election agent, whether before, during, or after an election, on account of or in respect of the conduct or management of such election, in excess of any maximum amount in that behalf specified in the first schedule to this Act.

(2.) Any candidate or election agent who knowingly acts in contravention of this section shall be guilty of an illegal practice.

Voting by Prohibited Persons and Publishing of False Statements of Withdrawal to be Illegal. **9.** (1.) If any person votes or induces or procures any person to vote at any election, knowing that he or such person is prohibited, whether by this or any other Act, from voting at such election, he shall be guilty of an illegal practice.

(2.) Any person who before or during an election knowingly

publishes a false statement of the withdrawal of a candidate at such election for the purpose of promoting or procuring the election of another candidate shall be guilty of an illegal practice.

(3.) Provided that a candidate shall not be liable, nor shall his election be avoided, for any illegal practice under this section committed by his agent other than his election agent. *Punishment on conviction of Illegal Practice.*

10. A person guilty of an illegal practice, whether under the foregoing sections or under the provisions hereinafter contained in this Act, shall on summary conviction be liable to a fine not exceeding one hundred pounds and be incapable during a period of five years from the date of his conviction of being registered as an elector or voting at any election (whether it be a parliamentary election or an election for a public office within the meaning of this Act) held for or within the county or borough in which the illegal practice has been committed.

11. Whereas by sub-section fourteen of section eleven of the Parliamentary Elections Act, 1868, it is provided that where a charge is made in an election petition of any corrupt practice having been committed at the election to which the petition refers, the judge shall report in writing to the Speaker as follows :— *Report of Election Court respecting Illegal Practice and Punishment of Candidate found guilty by such Report.*

(*a*.) " Whether any corrupt practice has or has not been " proved to have been committed by or with the " knowledge and consent of any candidate at such " election, and the nature of such corrupt practice ;

(*b*.) " The names of all persons, if any, who have been " proved at the trial to have been guilty of any corrupt " practice ;

(*c*.) " Whether corrupt practices have, or whether there is " reason to believe corrupt practices have, extensively " prevailed at the election to which the petition re- " lates " :

And whereas it is expedient to extend the said sub-section to illegal practices:

Be it therefore enacted as follows :—

Sub-section fourteen of section eleven of the Parliamentary Elections Act, 1868, shall apply as if that sub-section were herein re-enacted with the substitution of illegal practice within the meaning of this Act for corrupt practice ; and upon the trial of an election petition respecting an election for a county or borough, the election court shall report in writing to the Speaker the particulars required by the said sub-section as herein re-enacted, and shall also report whether any candidate at such election has been guilty by his agents of any illegal practice within the meaning of this Act in reference to such election, and the following consequences shall ensue upon the report by the election court to the Speaker ; (that is to say,)

> (*a*.) If the report is that any illegal practice has been proved to have been committed in reference to such election by or with the knowledge and consent of any candidate at such election, that candidate shall not be capable of being elected to or sitting in the House of Commons for the said county or borough for seven years next after the date of the report, and if he has been elected his election shall be void ; and he shall further be subject to the same incapacities as if at the date of the report he had been convicted of such illegal practice; and
>
> (*b*.) If the report is that a candidate at such election has been guilty by his agents of any illegal practice in reference to such election, that candidate shall not be capable of being elected to or sitting in the House of Commons for the said county or borough during the Parliament for which the election was held, and if he has been elected, his election shall be void.

12. Whereas by the Election Commissioners Act, 1852, as amended by the Parliamentary Elections Act, 1868, it is enacted that where a joint address of both Houses of Parliament represents to her Majesty that an election court has reported to the Speaker that corrupt practices have, or that there is reason to believe that corrupt practices have, extensively prevailed at an election in any county or borough, and prays her Majesty to cause inquiry under that Act to be made by persons named in such address (being qualified as therein mentioned), it shall be lawful for her Majesty to appoint the said persons to be election commissioners for the purpose of making inquiry into the existence of such corrupt practices :

Extension of 15 and 16 Vict., c. 57, respecting Election Commissioners to Illegal Practices. 15 and 16 Vict., c. 57, 31 and 32 Vict., c. 125.

And whereas it is expedient to extend the said enactments to the case of illegal practices :

Be it therefore enacted as follows :—

When election commissioners have been appointed in pursuance of the Election Commissioners Act, 1852, and the enactments amending the same, they may make inquiries and act and report as if " corrupt practices " in the said Act and the enactments amending the same included illegal practices ; and the Election Commissioners Act, 1852, shall be construed with such modifications as are necessary for giving effect to this section, and the expression " corrupt practice " in that Act shall have the same meaning as in this Act.

Illegal Payment, Employment, and Hiring.

13. Where a person knowingly provides money for any payment which is contrary to the provisions of this Act, or for any expenses incurred in excess of any maximum amount allowed by this Act, or for replacing any money expended in any such payment or expenses, except where the same may

Providing of Money for Illegal Practice or Payment to be Illegal Payment.

have been previously allowed in pursuance of this Act to be an exception. such person shall be guilty of illegal payment.

Employment of Hackney Carriages, or of Carriages and Horses kept for hire.

14. (1.) A person shall not let, lend, or employ for the purpose of the conveyance of electors to or from the poll, any public stage or hackney carriage, or any horse or other animal kept or used for drawing the same, or any carriage, horse, or other animal which he keeps or uses for the purpose of letting out for hire, and if he lets, lends, or employs such carriage, horse, or other animal, knowing that it is intended to be used for the purpose of the conveyance of electors to or from the poll, he shall be guilty of an illegal hiring.

(2.) A person shall not hire, borrow, or use for the purpose of the conveyance of electors to or from the poll any carriage, horse, or other animal which he knows the owner thereof is prohibited by this section to let, lend, or employ for that purpose, and if he does so he shall be guilty of an illegal hiring.

(3.) Nothing in this Act shall prevent a carriage, horse, or other animal being let to or hired, employed, or used by any elector, or several electors at their joint cost, for the purpose of being conveyed to or from the poll.

(4.) No person shall be liable to pay any duty or to take out a license for any carriage by reason only of such carriage being used without payment or promise of payment for the conveyance of electors to or from the poll at an election.

Corrupt Withdrawal from a Candidature.

15. Any person who corruptly induces or procures any other person to withdraw from being a candidate at an election, in consideration of any payment or promise of payment, shall be guilty of illegal payment, and any person withdrawing. in pursuance of such inducement or procurement, shall also be guilty of illegal payment.

Certain Expenditure to be Illegal Payment.

16. (1.) No payment or contract for payment shall, for the purpose of promoting or procuring the election of a candidate at any election, be made on account of bands of music, torches, flags, banners, cockades, ribbons, or other marks of distinction.

(2.) Subject to such exception as may be allowed in pursuance of this Act, if any payment or contract for payment is made in contravention of this section, either before, during, or after an election, the person making such payment shall be guilty of illegal payment, and any person being a party to any such contract or receiving such payment shall also be guilty of illegal payment if he knew that the same was made contrary to law.

17. (1.) No person shall, for the purpose of promoting or procuring the election of a candidate at any election, be engaged or employed for payment or promise of payment for any purpose or in any capacity whatever, except for any purposes or capacities mentioned in the first or second parts of the First Schedule to this Act, or except so far as payment is authorised by the first or second parts of the First Schedule to this Act. *Certain Employment to be Illegal.*

(2.) Subject to such exception as may be allowed in pursuance of this Act, if any person is engaged or employed in contravention of this section, either before, during, or after an election, the person engaging or employing him shall be guilty of illegal employment, and the person so engaged or employed shall also be guilty of illegal employment if he knew that he was engaged or employed contrary to law.

18. Every bill, placard, or poster having reference to an election shall bear upon the face thereof the name and address of the printer and publisher thereof; and any person printing, publishing, or posting, or causing to be printed, published, or posted, any such bill, placard, or poster as aforesaid, which fails to bear upon the face thereof the name and address of the printer and publisher, shall, if he is the candidate, or the election agent of the candidate, be guilty of an illegal practice, and if he is not the candidate, or the election agent of a can- *Name and Address of Printer on Placards.*

didate, shall be liable on summary conviction to a fine not exceeding one hundred pounds.

Saving for Creditors. **19.** The provisions of this Act prohibiting certain payments and contracts for payments, and the payment of any sum, and the incurring of any expense in excess of a certain maximum, shall not affect the right of any creditor, who, when the contract was made or the expense was incurred, was ignorant of the same being in contravention of this Act.

Use of Committee-room in house for Sale of Intoxicating Liquor or Refreshment to be Illegal Hiring. **20.** (*a.*) Any premises on which the sale by wholesale or retail of any intoxicating liquor is authorised by a license (whether the license be for consumption on or off the premises), or

(*b.*) Any premises where any intoxicating liquor is sold, or is supplied to members of a club, society, or association other than a permanent political club, or

(*c.*) Any premises whereon refreshment of any kind, whether food or drink, is ordinarily sold for consumption on the premises, or

(*d.*) The premises of any public elementary school in receipt of an annual parliamentary grant, or any part of any such premises, shall not be used as a committee-room for the purpose of promoting or procuring the election of a candidate at an election, and if any person hires or uses any such premises or any part thereof for a committee-room he shall be guilty of illegal hiring, and the person letting such premises or part, if he knew it was intended to use the same as a committee-room, shall also be guilty of illegal hiring :

Provided that nothing in this section shall apply to any part of such premises which is ordinarily let for the purpose of chambers or offices or the holding of public meetings or of arbitrations. if such part has a separate entrance and no direct communication with any part of the premises on which any intoxicating liquor or refreshment is sold or supplied as aforesaid.

21. (1.) A person guilty of an offence of illegal payment, employment, or hiring shall, on summary conviction, be liable to a fine not exceeding one hundred pounds.

(2.) A candidate or an election agent of a candidate who is personally guilty of an offence of illegal payment, employment, or hiring shall be guilty of an illegal practice.

Punishment of Illegal Payment, Employment, or Hiring.

Excuse and Exception for Corrupt or Illegal Practice or Illegal Payment, Employment, or Hiring.

22. Where, upon the trial of an election petition respecting an election for a county or borough, the election court report that a candidate at such election has been guilty by his agents of the offence of treating and undue influence, and illegal practice, or of any of such offences, in reference to such election, and the election court further report that the candidate has proved to the court —

Report exonerating Candidate in certain cases of Corrupt and Illegal Practice by Agents.

(a.) That no corrupt or illegal practice was committed at such election by the candidate or his election agent and the offences mentioned in the said report were committed contrary to the orders and without the sanction or connivance of such candidate or his election agent ; and

(b.) That such candidate and his election agent took all reasonable means for preventing the commission of corrupt and illegal practices at such election ; and

(c.) That the offences mentioned in the said report were of a trivial, unimportant, and limited character ; and

(d.) That in all other respects the election was free from any corrupt or illegal practice on the part of such candidate and of his agents ;

then the election of such candidate shall not, by reason of the offences mentioned in such report, be void, nor shall the candidate be subject to any incapacity under this Act.

M

Power of.
High
Court and
Election
Court to
except
innocent
act from
being
Illegal
Practice

23. Where, on application made, it is shown to the High Court or to an election court by such evidence as seems to the Court sufficient—

(*a*.) that any act or omission of a candidate at any election, or of his election agent or of any other agent or person, would, by reason of being a payment, engagement, employment, or contract in contravention of this Act, or being the payment of a sum or the incurring of expense in excess of any maximum amount allowed by this Act, or of otherwise being in contravention of any of the provisions of this Act, be but for this section an illegal practice, payment, employment, or hiring; and

(*b*.) that such act or omission arose from inadvertence or from accidental miscalculation or from some other reasonable cause of a like nature, and in any case did not arise from any want of good faith; and

(*c*.) that such notice of the application has been given in the county or borough for which the election was held as to the court seems fit;

and under the circumstances it seems to the Court to be just that the candidate and the said election and other agent and person, or any of them, should not be subject to any of the consequences under this Act of the said act or omission, the Court may make an order allowing such act or omission to be an exception from the provisions of this Act which would otherwise make the same an illegal practice, payment, employment, or hiring, and thereupon such candidate, agent, or person shall not be subject to any of the consequences under this Act of the said act or omission.

Election Expenses.

Nomina-
tion of
Election
Agent.

24. (1.) On or before the day of nomination at an election, a person shall be named by or on behalf of each candidate as his agent for such election (in this Act referred to as the election agent).

(2.) A candidate may name himself as election agent, and thereupon shall, so far as circumstances admit, be subject to the provisions of this Act both as a candidate and as an election agent, and any reference in this Act to an election agent shall be construed to refer to the candidate acting in his capacity of election agent.

(3.) On or before the day of nomination the name and address of the election agent of each candidate shall be declared in writing by the candidate or some other person on his behalf to the returning officer, and the returning officer shall forthwith give public notice of the name and address of every election agent so declared.

(4.) One election agent only shall be appointed for each candidate, but the appointment, whether the election agent appointed be the candidate himself or not, may be revoked, and in the event of such revocation or his death, whether such event is before, during, or after the election, then forthwith another election agent shall be appointed, and his name and address declared in writing to the returning officer, who shall forthwith give public notice of the same.

25. (1.) In the case of the elections specified in that behalf in the first schedule to this Act an election agent of a candidate may appoint the number of deputies therein mentioned (which deputies are in this Act referred to as sub-agents), to act within different polling districts. *Nomination of Deputy Election Agent as Sub-agent.*

(2.) As regards matters in a polling district the election agent may act by the sub-agent for that district, and anything done for the purposes of this Act by or to the sub-agent in his district shall be deemed to be done by or to the election agent, and any act or default of a sub-agent which, if he were the election agent, would be an illegal practice or other offence against this Act, shall be an illegal practice and offence against this Act committed by the sub-agent, and the sub-agent shall be liable to punishment accordingly ; and the candidate shall suffer the like incapacity as if the said act or default had been the act or default of the election agent.

(3.) One clear day before the polling the election agent shall declare in writing the name and address of every sub-agent to the returning officer, and the returning officer shall forthwith give public notice of the name and address of every sub-agent so declared.

(4.) The appointment of a sub-agent shall not be vacated by the election agent who appointed him ceasing to be election agent, but may be revoked by the election agent for the time being of the candidate, and in the event of such revocation or of the death of a sub-agent another sub-agent shall be forthwith declared in writing to the returning officer, who shall forthwith give public notice of the same.

Office of Election Agent and Sub-Agent.

26. (1.) An election agent at an election for a county or borough shall have within the county or borough, or within any county of a city or town adjoining thereto, and a sub-agent shall have within his district, or within any county of a city or town adjoining thereto, an office or place to which all claims, notices, writs, summons, and documents may be sent, and the address of such office or place shall be declared at the same time as the appointment of the said agent to the returning officer, and shall be stated in the public notice of the name of the agent.

(2.) Any claim, notice, writ, summons, or document delivered at such office or place and addressed to the election agent or sub-agent, as the case may be, shall be deemed to have been served on him, and every such agent may in respect of any matter connected with the election in which he is acting be sued in any court having jurisdiction in the county or borough in which the said office or place is situate.

27. (1.) The election agent of a candidate by himself or by his sub-agent shall appoint every polling agent, clerk, and messenger employed for payment on behalf of the candidate at an election, and hire every committee-room hired on behalf of the candidate. *Making of Contracts through Election Agent.*

(2.) A contract whereby any expenses are incurred on account of or in respect of the conduct or management of an election shall not be enforceable against a candidate at such election unless made by the candidate himself or by his election agent, either by himself or by his sub-agent ; provided that the inability under this section to enforce such contract against the candidate shall not relieve the candidate from the consequences of any corrupt or illegal practice having been committed by his agent.

28. (1.) Except as permitted by or in pursuance of this Act, no payment and no advance or deposit shall be made by a candidate at an election or by any agent on behalf of the candidate or by any other person at any time, whether before, during, or after such election, in respect of any expenses incurred on account of or in respect of the conduct or management of such election, otherwise than by or through the election agent of the candidate, whether acting in person or by a sub-agent ; and all money provided by any person other than the candidate for any expenses incurred on account of or in respect of the conduct or management of the election, whether as gift, loan, advance, or deposit, shall be paid to the candidate or his election agent and not otherwise ; *Payment of Expenses through Election Agent.*

Provided that this section shall not be deemed to apply to a tender of security to or any payment by the returning officer or to any sum disbursed by any person out of his own money for any small expense legally incurred by himself, if such sum is not repaid to him.

(2.) A person who makes any payment, advance, or deposit in contravention of this section, or pays in contravention of this section any money so provided as aforesaid, shall be guilty of an illegal practice.

29. (1.) Every payment made by an election agent, whether by himself or a sub-agent, in respect of any expenses incurred on account of or in respect of the conduct or management of an election, shall, except where less than forty shillings, be vouched for by a bill stating the particulars, and by a receipt.

(2.) Every claim against a candidate at an election or his election agent in respect of any expenses incurred on account of or in respect of the conduct or management of such election which is not sent in to the election agent within the time limited by this Act shall be barred and shall not be paid; and, subject to such exception as may be allowed in pursuance of this Act, an election agent who pays a claim in contravention of this enactment shall be guilty of an illegal practice.

(3.) Except as by this Act permitted, the time limited by this Act for sending in claims shall be fourteen days after the day on which the candidates returned are declared elected.

(4.) All expenses incurred by or on behalf of a candidate at an election, which are incurred on account of or in respect of the conduct or management of such election, shall be paid within the time limited by this Act and not otherwise; and, subject to such exception as may be allowed in pursuance of this Act, an election agent who makes a payment in contravention of this provision shall be guilty of an illegal practice.

(5.) Except as by this Act permitted, the time limited by this Act for the payment of such expenses as aforesaid shall be twenty-eight days after the day on which the candidates returned are declared elected.

(6.) Where the election court reports that it has been proved to such court by a candidate that any payment made by an election agent in contravention of this section was made without the sanction or connivance of such candidate, the election of such candidate shall not be void, nor shall he be subject to any incapacity under this Act by reason only of such payment having been made in contravention of this section.

(7.) If the election agent in the case of any claim sent in to him within the time limited by this Act disputes it, or refuses or fails to pay it within the said period of twenty-eight days, such claim shall be deemed to be a disputed claim.

(8.) The claimant may, if he thinks fit, bring an action for a disputed claim in any competent court ; and any sum paid by the candidate or his agent in pursuance of the judgment or order of such court shall be deemed to be paid within the time limited by this Act, and to be an exception from the provisions of this Act, requiring claims to be paid by the election agent.

(9) On cause shown to the satisfaction of the High Court, such court on application by the claimant or by the candidate or his election agent may by order give leave for the payment by a candidate or his election agent of a disputed claim, or of a claim for any such expenses as aforesaid, although sent in after the time in this section mentioned for sending in claims, or although the same was sent in to the candidate and not to the election agent.

(10.) Any sum specified in the order of leave may be paid by the candidate or his election agent, and when paid in pursuance of such leave shall be deemed to be paid within the time limited by this Act.

Reference to Taxation of Claim against Candidates.

30. If any action is brought in any competent court to recover a disputed claim against a candidate at an election, or his election agent, in respect of any expenses incurred on account or in respect of the conduct or management of such election, and the defendant admits his liability, but disputes the amount of the claim, the said amount shall, unless the court, on the application of the plaintiff in the action, otherwise directs, be forthwith referred for taxation to the master, official referee, registrar, or other proper officer of the court, and the amount found due on such taxation shall be the amount to be recovered in such action in respect of such claim.

Personal Expenses of Candidate and Petty Expenses.

31. (1.) The candidate at an election may pay any personal expenses incurred by him on account of or in connexion with or incidental to such election to an amount not exceeding one hundred pounds, but any further personal expenses so incurred by him shall be paid by his election agent.

(2.) The candidate shall send to the election agent within the time limited by this Act for sending in claims a written statement of the amount of personal expenses paid as aforesaid by such candidate.

(3.) Any person may, if so authorized in writing by the election agent of the candidate, pay any necessary expenses for stationery, postage, telegrams, and other petty expenses, to a total amount not exceeding that named in the authority, but any excess above the total amount so named shall be paid by the election agent.

(4.) A statement of the particulars of payments made by any person so authorized shall be sent to the election agent within the time limited by this Act for the sending in of claims, and shall be vouched for by a bill containing the receipt of that person.

32. (1.) So far as circumstances admit, this Act shall apply to a claim for his remuneration by an election agent and to the payment thereof in like manner as if he were any other creditor, and if any difference arises respecting the amount of such claim the claim shall be a disputed claim within the meaning of this Act, and be dealt with accordingly. Remuneration of Election Agent and Returning Officer's Expenses.

(2.) The account of the charges claimed by the returning officer in the case of a candidate and transmitted in pursuance of section four of the Parliamentary Elections (Returning Officers) Act, 1875, shall be transmitted within the time specified in the said section to the election agent of the candidate, and need not be transmitted to the candidate.

33. (1.) Within thirty-five days after the day on which the candidates returned at an election are declared elected, the election agent of every candidate at that election shall transmit to the returning officer a true return (in this Act referred to as a return respecting election expenses), in the form set forth in the Second Schedule to this Act or to the like effect, containing, as respects that candidate — Return and Declaration respecting Election Expenses.

(a.) A statement of all payments made by the election agent, together with all the bills and receipts (which bills and receipts are in this Act included in the expression " return respecting election expenses ") ;

(b.) A statement of the amount of personal expenses, if any, paid by the candidate ;

(c.) A statement of the sums paid to the returning officer for his charges, or, if the amount is in dispute, of the sum claimed, and the amount disputed ;

(d.) A statement of all other disputed claims of which the election agent is aware ;

(e.) A statement of all the unpaid claims, if any, of which the election agent is aware, in respect of which application has been or is about to be made to the High Court ;

(*f.*) A statement of all money, securities, and equivalent of money received by the election agent from the candidate or any other person for the purpose of expenses incurred or to be incurred on account of or in respect of the conduct or management of the election, with a statement of the name of every person from whom the same may have been received.

(2.) The return so transmitted to the returning officer shall be accompanied by a declaration made by the election agent before a justice of the peace in the form in the Second Schedule to this Act (which declaration is in this Act referred to as a declaration respecting election expenses).

(3.) Where the candidate has named himself as his election agent, a statement of all money, securities, and equivalent of money paid by the candidate shall be substituted in the return required by this section to be transmitted by the election agent for the like statement of money, securities, and equivalent of money received by the election agent from the candidate ; and the declaration by an election agent respecting election expenses need not be made, and the declaration by the candidate respecting election expenses shall be modified as specified in the Second Schedule to this Act.

(4.) At the same time that the agent transmits the said return, or within seven days afterwards, the candidate shall transmit or cause to be transmitted to the returning officer a declaration made by him before a justice of the peace, in the form in the first part of the Second Schedule to this Act (which declaration is in this Act referred to as a declaration respecting election expenses).

(5.) If in the case of an election for any county or borough, the said return and declarations are not transmitted before the expiration of the time limited for the purpose, the candidate shall not, after the expiration of such time, sit or vote in the House of Commons as member for that county or borough until either such return and declarations have been transmitted, or until the date of the allowance of such an authorized excuse for the failure to transmit the same, as in this Act mentioned, and if he sits or votes in contravention of this enactment he shall forfeit one hundred pounds for every day on which he so sits or votes to any person who sues for the same.

(6.) If without such authorized excuse as in this Act mentioned, a candidate or an election agent fails to comply with the requirements of this section he shall be guilty of an illegal practice.

(7.) If any candidate or election agent knowingly makes the declaration required by this section falsely, he shall be guilty of an offence, and on conviction thereof on indictment shall be liable to the punishment for wilful and corrupt perjury; such offence shall also be deemed to be a corrupt practice within the meaning of this Act.

(8.) Where the candidate is out of the United Kingdom at the time when the return is so transmitted to the returning officer, the declaration required by this section may be made by him within fourteen days after his return to the United Kingdom, and in that case shall be forthwith transmitted to the returning officer, but the delay hereby authorized in making such declaration shall not exonerate the election agent from complying with the provisions of this Act as to the return and declaration respecting election expenses.

(9.) Where, after the date at which the return respecting election expenses is transmitted, leave is given by the High Court for any claims to be paid, the candidate or his election agent shall, within seven days after the payment thereof, transmit to the returning officer a return of the sums paid in pursuance of such leave accompanied by a copy of the order of the Court giving the leave, and in default he shall be deemed to have failed to comply with the requirements of this section without such authorized excuse as in this Act mentioned.

Authorized excuse for non-compliance with Provisions as to Return and Declaration of Election Expenses.

34. (1.) Where the return and declarations respecting election expenses of a candidate at an election for a county or borough have not been transmitted as required by this Act, or being transmitted contain some error or false statement, then —

(*a*.) if the candidate applies to the High Court or an election court and shows that the failure to transmit such return and declarations, or any of them, or any part thereof, or any error or false statement therein, has arisen by reason of his illness, or of the absence, death, illness, or misconduct of his election agent or sub-agent or of any clerk or officer of such agent, or by reason of inadvertence or of any reasonable cause of a like nature, and not by reason of any want of good faith on the part of the applicant, or

(*b*.) if the election agent of the candidate applies to the High Court or an election court and shows that the failure to transmit the return and declarations which he was required to transmit, or any part thereof, or any error or false statement therein, arose by reason of his illness or of the death or illness of any prior election agent of the candidate, or of the absence, death, illness, or misconduct of any sub-agent, clerk, or officer of an election agent of the candidate, or by reason of inadvertence or of any reasonable cause of a like nature, and not by reason of any want of good faith on the part of the applicant,

the Court may, after such notice of the application in the said county or borough, and on production of such evidence of the grounds stated in the application, and of the good faith of the application, and otherwise, as to the Court seems fit, make such order for allowing an authorized excuse for the failure to transmit such return and declaration, or for an error or false statement in such return and declaration, as to the Court seems just.

(2.) Where it appears to the Court that any person being or having been an election agent or sub-agent has refused or failed to make such return or to supply such particulars as will enable the candidate and his election agent respectively to comply with the provisions of this Act as to the return and declaration respecting election expenses, the Court before making an order allowing the excuse as in this section mentioned shall order such person to attend before the Court, and on his attendance shall, unless he shows cause to the contrary, order him to make the return and declaration, or to deliver a statement of the particulars required to be contained in the return, as to the Court seem just, and to make or deliver the same within such time and to such person and in such manner as the Court may direct, or may order him to be examined with respect to such particulars, and may in default of compliance with any such order order him to pay a fine not exceeding five hundred pounds.

(3.) The order may make the allowance conditional upon the making of the return and declaration in a modified form or within an extended time, and upon the compliance with such other terms as to the Court seem best calculated for carrying into effect the objects of this Act ; and an order allowing an authorized excuse shall relieve the applicant for the order from any liability or consequences under this Act in respect of the matter excused by the order; and where it is proved by the candidate to the Court that any act or omission of the election agent in relation to the return and declaration respecting election expenses was without the sanction or connivance of the candidate, and that the candidate took all reasonable means for preventing such act or omission, the Court shall relieve the candidate from the consequences of such act or omission on the part of his election agent.

(4.) The date of the order, or if conditions and terms are to be complied with, the date at which the applicant fully complies with them, is referred to in this Act as the date of the allowance of the excuse.

Publication of Summary of Return of Election Expenses.

35. (1.) The returning officer at an election within ten days after he receives from the election agent of a candidate a return respecting election expenses shall publish a summary of the return in not less than two newspapers circulating in the county or borough for which the election was held, accompanied by a notice of the time and place at which the return and declarations (including the accompanying documents) can be inspected, and may charge the candidate in respect of such publication, and the amount of such charge shall be the sum allowed by the Parliamentary Elections (Returning Officers) Act, 1875.

(2.) The return and declarations (including the accompanying documents) sent to the returning officer by an election agent shall be kept at the office of the returning officer, or some convenient place appointed by him, and shall at all reasonable times during two years next after they are received by the returning officer be open to inspection by any person on payment of a fee of one shilling, and the returning officer shall on demand furnish copies thereof or any part thereof at the price of twopence for every seventy-two words. After the expiration of the said two years the returning officer may cause the said return and declarations (including the accompanying documents) to be destroyed, or, if the candidate or his election agent so require, shall return the same to the candidate.

First Schedule.

PART I.

Persons Legally Employed for Payment.

(1.) One election agent and no more.

(2.) In counties one deputy election agent (in this Act referred to as a sub-agent) to act within each polling district and no more.

(3.) One polling agent in each polling station and no more.

(4.) In a borough one clerk and one messenger, or if the number of electors in the borough exceeds five hundred, a number of clerks and messengers not exceeding in number one clerk and one messenger for every complete five hundred electors in the borough, and if there is a number of electors over and above any complete five hundred or complete five hundreds of electors, then one clerk and one messenger may be employed for such number, although not amounting to a complete five hundred.

(5.) In a county for the central committee-room one clerk and one messenger, or if the number of electors in the county exceeds five thousand, then a number of clerks and messengers not exceeding in number one clerk and one messenger for every complete five thousand electors in the county; and if there is a number of electors over and above any complete five thousand or complete five thousands of electors, then one clerk and one messenger may be employed for such number, although not amounting to a complete five thousand.

(6.) In a county a number of clerks and messengers not exceeding in number one clerk and one messenger for each polling district in the county, or where the number of electors in a polling district exceeds five hundred one clerk and one messenger for every complete five hundred electors in the polling district, and if there is a number of electors over and above any complete five hundred or complete five hundreds of electors, then one clerk and one messenger may be employed for such number, although not amounting to a complete five hundred: Provided always, that the number of clerks and messengers so allowed in any county may be employed in any polling district where their services may be required.

(7.) Any such paid election agent, sub-agent, polling agent, clerk, and messenger may or may not be an elector but may not vote.

*　　　*　　　*　　　*　　　*

PART II.

Legal Expenses in Addition to Expenses under Part I.

(1.) Sums paid to the returning officer for his charges not exceeding the amount authorized by the Act 38 and 39 Vict. c. 84.

(2.) The personal expenses of the candidate.

(3.) The expenses of printing, the expenses of advertising, and the expenses of publishing, issuing, and distributing addresses and notices.

(4.) The expenses of stationery, messages, postage, and telegrams.

(5.) The expenses of holding public meetings.

(6.) In a borough the expenses of one committee-room and if the number of electors in the borough exceeds five hundred then of a number of committee-rooms not exceeding the number of one committee-room for every complete five hundred electors in the borough, and if there is a number of electors over and above any complete five hundred or complete five hundreds of electors, then of one committee-room for such number, although not amounting to a complete five hundred.

(7.) In a county the expenses of a central committee-room, and in addition of a number of committee-rooms not exceeding in number one committee-room for each polling district in the county, and where the number of electors in a polling district exceeds five hundred one additional committee-room may be hired for every complete five hundred electors in such polling district over and above the first five hundred.

PART III.

MAXIMUM FOR MISCELLANEOUS MATTERS.

Expenses in respect of miscellaneous matters other than those mentioned in Part I. and Part II. of this schedule not exceeding in the whole the maximum amount of two hundred pounds, so nevertheless that such expenses are not incurred in respect of any matter or in any manner constituting an offence under this or any other Act, or in respect of any matter or thing, payment for which is expressly prohibited by this or any other Act.

PART IV.

MAXIMUM SCALE.

(1.) In a borough the expenses mentioned above in Parts I., II., and III. of this schedule, other than personal expenses and sums paid to the returning officer for his charges, shall not exceed in the whole the maximum amount in the scale following :—

If the number of electors on the register—

The maximum amount shall be—

Does not exceed 2,000 . £350.

Exceeds 2,000 . . . . £380, and an additional £30 for every complete 1,000 electors above 2,000.

N

Provided that in Ireland if
the number of electors   The maximum amount shall
on the register—   be—
    Does not exceed 500 . . £200.
    Exceeds 500, but does not
      exceed 1,000 . . . . £250.
    Exceeds 1,000, but does not
      exceed 1,500 . . . £275.

(2.) In a county the expenses mentioned above in Parts I., II., and III. of this schedule, other than personal expenses and sums paid to the returning officer for his charges, shall not exceed in the whole the maximum amount in the scale following :—

If the number of electors   The maximum amount shall
on the register—   be—
    Does not exceed 2,000 . . £650 in England and Scotland, and £500 in Ireland.

    Exceeds 2,000 . . . . £710 in England and Scotland, and £540 in Ireland ; and an additional £60 in England and Scotland, and £40 in Ireland, for every complete 1,000 electors above 2,000.

SUMMARY OF ELECTION OFFENCES.

OFFENCES.	PENALTIES.

CORRUPT PRACTICES.

BRIBERY.—No gift, loan, or promise of money or money's worth must be made to a voter to induce him either to vote or abstain from voting.

The offer or promise of a situation or employment to a voter or anyone connected with him, if made with the same object, is also bribery.

The consequences are the same whether bribery is committed before, during, or after an election.

Giving or paying money for the purpose of bribery is equivalent to the offence itself.

A gift or promise to a third person to procure a vote is bribery. Payment for loss of time, wages, or travelling expenses is equal to bribery.

Any person who receives a bribe, or bargains for employment or reward in consideration of his vote, is guilty of bribery.

To the briber or the person bribed, twelve months' imprisonment, with or without hard labour, or a fine of £200.

Deprivation of the right of voting for seven years.

Removal from, and disqualification for, any public office.

Payment of costs of an election inquiry in certain cases.

If committed by the candidate he also loses his seat, if elected, and is disqualified for ever from representing the constituency.

If committed by any agent the election is void, and the candidate is disqualified for seven years.

TREATING.—No meat, drink, entertainment or provision can be paid for or provided for any person, at any time, in order to induce him, or any other person, to vote or abstain from voting.

Treating the wives or relatives of voters is equally forbidden.

The gift of tickets to be exchanged for refreshment is treating.

The receiver of any meat, drink, etc., is equally guilty, and liable to the same consequences.

The same as for bribery.

UNDUE INFLUENCE—No force, restraint, or fraud may be used to compel an elector to vote or abstain.

Using or threatening any spiritual or temporal injury is undue influence.

The withdrawal of custom, or a threat to do so, comes under this prohibition. A threat to evict a tenant will also be undue influence.

The same as for bribery.

PERSONATION.—*Applying for* a ballot paper in the name of another person, whether live or dead.

Voting twice at the same election.

Aiding or abetting the commission of the offence of personation.

Forging or counterfeiting a ballot paper.

To the offender, two years' imprisonment, with hard labour.

Seven years' incapacity to vote, or hold any public office.

If committed by any agent, the candidate loses his seat.

ILLEGAL PRACTICES.

CONVEYANCE.—Paying *or receiving* money for conveyance of voters to or from the poll. (Private conveyances lent gratuitously can alone be employed; hackney carriages are prohibited except when hired by voters for their own exclusive use.)

ADVERTISING.—Paying money to an elector for exhibiting bills, &c. The *receiver* is also guilty.

COMMITTEE-ROOMS.—Hiring unauthorized committee-rooms. (The election agent *alone*, or sub-agents in counties, may hire committee-rooms, and the number is strictly limited.)

VOTING when prohibited, or inducing a prohibited elector to vote. (Electors employed for payment cannot vote.)

FALSE STATEMENT.—Publishing a false statement of the withdrawal of any candidate.

A fine of £100.
Incapacity to vote for five years.
If committed by an agent, the election may be rendered void.

ILLEGAL PAYMENT, EMPLOYMENT, AND HIRING.

PUBLISHING BILLS. placards, or posters without the printer's name and address. (The election agent *alone*, or sub-agents in counties, must issue any printed matter at the election.)

PAYMENT FOR BANDS OF MUSIC, torches, flags, banners, ribbons, &c.

LENDING OR USING, for the conveyance of voters, horses or vehicles usually kept for hire.

EMPLOYMENT of any persons beyond the numbers allowed. (No person can be employed for payment at an election except by the election agent, or sub-agents in counties, who is strictly limited as to the numbers he may engage.)

USING A COMMITTEE-ROOM in any licensed house, refreshment house, or public elementary school.

A fine of £100.

IMPORTANT.

Any of the above offences, if committed by a candidate, election agent (or sub-agent in counties), will render the election void.

The term "agent" as used above includes members of an election committee.

No expense must be incurred by anybody without the election agent's written authority, as the maximum expense allowed by law for each candidate cannot be exceeded without rendering the election void.

The person incurring any unauthorized expense will be personally liable for its repayment, as well as for the consequences of having broken the law.

INDEX.

A.

D.

E.

N.

O

T.

TREATING.

>By canvassers, 101.
>What is, 150.

U.

UNDUE INFLUENCE.

>What is, 151.

V.

VACANCIES, Causes of, 5, 6.
VACANCY.

>When commences, 42.

VEHICLES. (*See* Conveyances.)
VOLUNTARY ASSISTANCE.

>In preparing canvass books, etc., 22.

VOTERS.

>Doubtful, to have special attention, 62.
>In outlying districts, canvass of, 63.
>Illegal to pay travelling expenses of, 93, 139, 153.
>   „   „   „   „   „ except by sea in certain cases, 93.
>Interference with, on day of poll, 102.
>Polling of removed, 92, 138.
>Who are prohibited, 147.

VOTES, COUNTING OF.

>A simple method, 78.

VOTING, prohibited, 147, 148, 153.

W.

WARD COMMITTEES.

>Who should convene, 122.
>Election agent to attend meetings of, 123.
>Responsibility of individual members, 123.
>Meetings of, prior to polling day, 125.
>Duties of, on polling day, 127.

WITHDRAWAL.

>Publishing false statement of, an illegal practice, 154.
>Candidate not liable for false statement by agent other than election
>>agent, 155.

>Corrupt, 158.

www.ingramcontent.com/pod-product-compliance
Lightning Source LLC
Chambersburg PA
CBHW020623030726
47497CB00007B/2381